D0593351

EX LIBRIS

For Orion

Merry Christmas 2003!

Love, Dad

May you have much good luck
in your theatre work!

THEATRE

A CRASH COURSE

THEATRE

A CRASH COURSE

ROB GRAHAM

SIMON & SCHUSTER
A VIACOM COMPANY

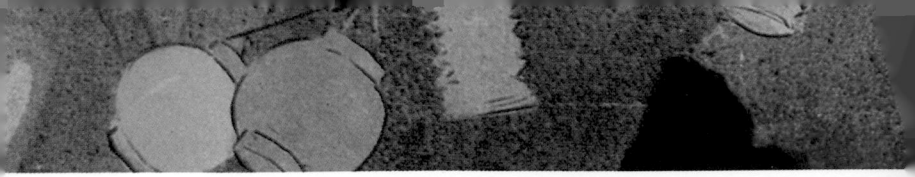

First published in Great Britain by
Simon & Schuster UK Ltd, 1999
A Viacom company

Copyright © THE IVY PRESS LIMITED 1999

This book is copyright under the Berne Convention
No reproduction without permission

All rights reserved. No part of this book may be reproduced, stored in a retrieval system, or transmitted, in any form or by any means, electronic, mechanical, photocopying, recording or otherwise, without prior permission in writing from the Publishers.

SIMON & SCHUSTER UK LTD
Africa House
64–78 Kingsway
London WC2B 6AH

SIMON & SCHUSTER AUSTRALIA
Sydney

A CIP catalogue record for this book is available from the British Library

ISBN 0-684-85836-3

This book was conceived, designed and produced by
THE IVY PRESS LIMITED
2/3 St Andrews Place
Lewes, East Sussex BN7 1UP

Editorial Director: SOPHIE COLLINS
Art Director: PETER BRIDGEWATER
Editor: GRAPEVINE PUBLISHING SERVICES
Designer: JANE LANAWAY
DTP Designer: CHRIS LANAWAY
Illustrations: MADELEINE HARDIE
Picture Research: VANESSA FLETCHER

Reproduction and Printing in Hong Kong by
Hong Kong Graphic and Printing Ltd.

DEDICATION

To Joe and Erin

Contents

Introduction 8

'That's the Last Time I Play Mammoth!'
Prehistory, cave paintings, ritual and dance 12

A Horus Line
Passion in the pyramids 14

Tragedy, Comedy and Haemorrhoids
The famous Greeks 16

'Never Work with Animals...'
Rome and panto 18

Here Comes the Passion Wagon
'It's all a Mystery to me...' 20

Pigs' Blood, Guts and Explosions
European Mysteries 22

Theatre? What Theatre?
Machiavelli and the Italian Renaissance 24

Slapstick, Dirty Old Men and Cuckolds
The Italian commedia dell'arte 26

Golden Age of Spain
Cervantes, de Vega, Calderón 28

Tudor Days
Ralph Roister Doister to Gorboduc 30

The Glory Days
The Burbages, Marlowe, Jonson 32

And Now... The Lad 'Imself
William Shakespeare 34

Blood and Madness
The jolly Jacobeans 36

Masque Makers to the Gentry
Jones and Jonson 38

Big Noses and Bad Manners
The Renaissance in France 40

Molière the Great
Innovative social comedy 42

Decadence and Women!
Restoration theatre 44

Herr Sachs Sucks
Teutonic popular theatre 46

The Brits on Tour
Browne, Kempe and the 'Englische Komödianten' 48

Baroque? Actors are Always Baroque!
Italian melodramma in perspective 50

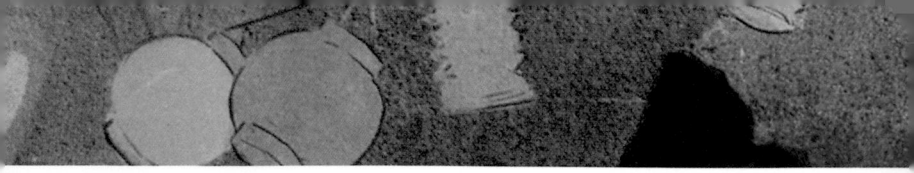

It's an *Epic* – So go to the Lav First!
India: Kalidasa, Shri-Harshadeva to Tagore 52

Wajang Gedog and the Shadows!
South-east Asia: marionettes and humans 54

Does Anyone Know What's Happening?
Things change slowly in Chinese theatre 56

No, No, not No... *Nō!*
Monkey music and Mannerism in Japan 58

Theatre, Revolution and Short Dictators
18th-century France: Voltaire, Beaumarchais, Talma and Napoleon 60

Meanwhile, in Venice ...
Papa Goldoni, Nasty Snr Gozzi and Alfieri 62

Sturm und Drang!
Von Klinger, Goethe and Schiller 64

Handsome Rogues
Cibber, Garrick, Sheridan, et al. 66

The Brits on Tour II: America
Kean & Murray, Hallam, Fennell and Cooper 68

The First Age of the American Actors
Payne, Forrest, the Booths and those Barrymores 70

Horrid Little Men
Kean, Kemble, Vestris 72

The Actor and the Manager
Macready, Phelps, Bancroft, Irving, Terry 74

Nationalism vs Naturalism
Büchner, Saxe-Meinengen, Wagner 76

Romanticism vs Naturalism
Hugo, De Musset, Sardou, Bernhardt and Antoine 78

Nationalism vs Everyone in Italy
D'Annunzio, Ristori, Duse, Salvini, 80

Scandinavian Mysticism
Ibsen and the split personality of Strindberg 82

Big Plays by Men with Big Facial Hair
Pushkin, Griboyedov, Gogol, Tolstoy and Chekhov 84

Melodrama, Disaster and the Follies!
America after the Civil War 86

From Russia with 'Loved You Darling!'
Stanislavski: the father of acting 88

Mysticism, Romance and Symbolism
The French and the Russians 90

Illogical and Unreal, but So Happy
The Futurists 92

Take Your Pick. We Got Naturalism...
Hauptmann, Gorky, O'Neill 94

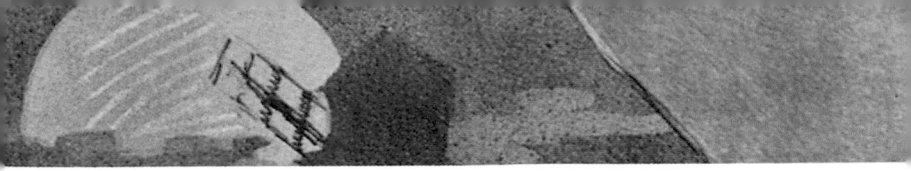

... Or We Got Realism
Europe and the States 96

Or If It's Been a Bad Hair Day...
How about Expressionism? 98

Jewels in the Dross
Irony and fantasy in England 100

Of Playboys and Gunmen
The Irish connection 102

A Shutter in the Dark
Craig, Appia, Wagner, Constructivism 104

Mad People and Modernists
From Dada to Ubu 106

Experiments Between Lenin and Hitler
Meyerhold, Piscator, Brecht 108

Happiness is... A Good Thrashing
The ecstasy and cruelty of Artaud and Grotowsky 110

Meanwhile, in Life's Waiting Room
Existentialism 112

The American Method
(Or how I stopped acting and learnt to mumble) 114

Stiff Upper Lip, Crease in your flannels
(Or a creased upper lip and a stiff in your flannels?) 116

Keep One's Vowels Regular!
Gielgud, Richardson, Olivier 118

Reviving the Corpse
Osborne, Devine, Wesker, Ayckbourn 120

Angry Young Persons
The revolutionaries 122

Tellin' It Like It Is
The American Realists 124

It's the Sixties! So Get Your Kit Off!
Hair and happenings 126

The Times, They Are A'Changin'
Agit-prop in the UK 128

Third World Voices
Apartheid and tyranny 130

Awakening Ex-Colonies
Australia and Canada 132

Blurring the Boundaries
Post-Modernism 134

Full Circle at Fin de Siècle?
Theatre returns to ritual and dance 136

Glossary 138

Old Thespian Sayings and Superstitions 140

Notable Performances 141

Index 142

Photographic Credits 144

Behind the Scenes
Theatre design, sets, staging, lighting, acting techniques and philosophies. The technical information that will enlighten you as to how it all takes shape, and ways in which it can go wrong.

Introduction

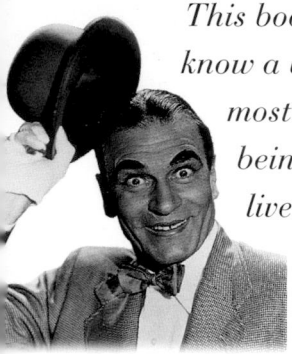

Larry camps it up as Archie Rice (1957), a trademark role.

This book is intended to help you know a bit more about one of the most wonderful activities human beings have ever dreamed up – live theatre. You probably already know quite a bit about its essence, even if you've never studied it. After all, putting funny hats on and pretending to be someone else is an integral part of most people's childhood (and no matter what any actor or director may loftily claim, theatre still operates partly at that level. As Laurence Olivier once said, 'it's no fit job for a grown man!'). Besides, acting is the greatest 'spectator sport' in the world, greater even than football!

Theatre has been with the human race virtually since it stood upright (I know, I know, there are still plenty of knuckles dragging on the floor). Although in this century it has had to move from centre stage to make room for radio, film

'This isn't what I trained for!' Actor pretending to be a mushroom.

and television, it hasn't gone to the wings to sulk. If anything, it just rushed off for yet another costume change. After modernism, theatre has found new ways of telling those stories we love to hear. Ways that try to celebrate all over again the wonder and magic of the 'live' performance unattainable by celluloid or videotape. Also, in the West it still provides the training ground for many actors, directors and writers, whilst in the emerging Third World it has yet again proved its superiority as an accessible means of voicing the pain, anger (and sometimes joy) of the growing numbers of dispossessed.

Timeline
More of a contextual chronology than a timeline, because writers, directors and movements are constantly overlapping. A highly idiosyncratic list of major and less major events happening at the time the protagonists were living, to illuminate the world they inhabited and the zeitgeist of the period.

'Darling, you're standing on my frock.' Sir Noel and Gertie Lawrence.

Its history and diversity is unbelievable. From tribal rituals to avant-garde performances; from religious festivals to well-made plays; from one-person shows to

PROMPT BOX

A useful little gem you can use to impress your luvvie friends: gossip, bitchiness, or the extra-curricular activities of some of the major names.

It's a miracle! Audiences loved these amateur religious shows.

casts of thousands; from short sketches to serious tests of bladder control; from light amusements to profound philosophy; from mild satire to something worth dying for; theatre has said and shown it all. There are two ways of making sense of life, religion and dramatic re-enactment, and sometimes even these get confused with each other (the clerical robes of office and the costume of the actor are not that far apart; and both can and do require the wearing of funny hats).

This book is necessarily selective in its attempt to convey the enormity of World theatre, and is sometimes opinionated and irreverent, but then so is theatre.

John Gielgud's classic *Hamlet* in 1933. Love the necklace, sweetie!

How this Course Works

Each double-page spread is devoted to a theatrical movement or a group of playwrights, actors or directors with something in common, and the story proceeds more or less chronologically. On each spread there are some regular features. It won't take you long to figure them out but check the boxes on pages 8-11 for more information.

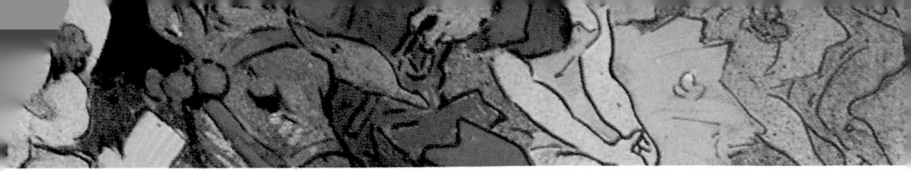

Actors like playing the Fool – not too many lines and they get all the laughs.

More than any other art form you care to mention, theatre is a dangerous business.

It is to governments and monarchies what Lear's fool was to Lear – an amusing idiot who often speaks the deepest of truths, no matter how painful or dangerous, and it is no accident that dictators take it very seriously. On the other hand, it is also used as a vehicle to promote the silliest and most pretentious notions imaginable, and has often been a refuge for certifiable lunatics. This book tries to convey the head, heart, guts, soul and toenail cuttings that make up theatre.

Supporting Roles

Other performers worthy of note alongside the major names (and often producing much more interesting work).

Rob Graham

ROB GRAHAM

Talking of lunatics... *Hair* featured hippy placards and nudity.

38000–5000 BC Cave paintings in Asia, Africa and Europe represent men and women dancing, probably one of the oldest forms of expression.

25000 BC Early Stone Age hunters start carving antler, bone and ivory, incising everyday implements, and making little figurines.

c. 7500 BC The domestic dog will become a hunting companion, a protector, an object of affection or loathing and a friend to humans and more than 400 breeds will be developed.

4000 BC

'That's the Last Time I Play Mammoth!'

Prehistory, cave paintings, ritual and dance

Before the Greeks and Romans, about whom we know relatively little, before the Egyptians, about whom we know even less, before, in fact, all that we refer to as 'ancient' theatre, how did folks enjoy a night out?

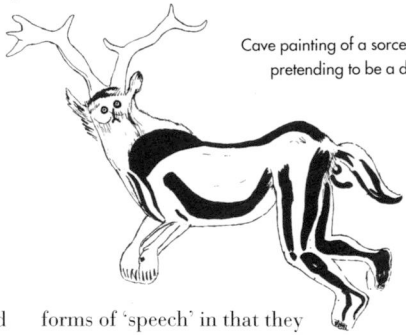

Cave painting of a sorceress pretending to be a deer.

In his *Poetics*, ARISTOTLE (384–322 BC) mentions ('Goes On A Lot About' would be nearer the mark) 'imitation' and how instinctive it is to the human race. Perhaps he was putting the case too strongly; it is probably more an aptitude than an instinct, but a powerful aptitude for all that. And this aptitude for imitation has been with us for a long time. We don't know who the first person was to find it fun to jump about in a mask or animal skin (nor do we know what his friends thought of him), but dance and the use of masks/costume must have developed alongside the earliest rituals. Both are forms of 'speech' in that they symbolically communicate emotional states too deep for words (or grunts).

Cave paintings in southern France clearly show men dressed 'as deer', as part of some hunting ritual (or a fashion statement?). Animal impersonation may well have been the earliest form of acting ('Mammoth in Boots'?).

PROMPT BOX

'Flyting' is the exchange of insults in a stylized manner. The Greeks used it, as did Shakespeare, and many modern writers. It has also formed the banter of much double-act comedy. Sometimes it is good-natured, other times not so. For example, barristers engage in a fair bit of nasty flyting, whilst politicians do little else.

00 BC The island of ete is occupied. The Minoan called after the legendary King Minos) Bronze Age culture will reach a peak in about 1600 BC, when it is destroyed by the Mycenaeans.

4400 BC The Halafians in Northern Syria construct circular domed buildings.

4000 BC The world's population reaches roughly 85 million.

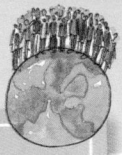

Supporting Roles

One ritual concerned the selection of the divine 'god-king-hero' to rule a community for one year. Then he was killed by a successor – who consequently inherited his sterling qualities and also ruled for a year until he was killed, and so on. (Might there have been a play entitled The Man Who Certainly Does Not Want To Be King, But Would Be Happy To Serve On The Selection Committee?).

The principal theories influencing our notions of ritual were formed by a group of wild things called the 'Cambridge school' at the turn of this century, and most notably by James Frazer in *The Golden Bough* (1890), and Jane Harrison in *Themis* (1912). These scholars, supported by studies in the history of religion, archaeology, anthropology etc., argued that early rituals were enacted to ensure social well being. Although they probably didn't get out enough, they had a point. Ritual has always been one of the keystones of theatre history. Like theatre, ritual emphasizes the doing of things – the concrete and the actual rather than the merely metaphysical. However, unlike theatre, which merely says a few things about social relationships, ritual reinforces or changes them.

Bronze cult wagon from the seventh century BC showing more strange deer rituals.

The central preoccupations of early rituals seems to have been maintaining order, sex, planting/harvesting crops, sex, new year celebrations, sex, the installation of a king and generally controlling the universe. Oh, and sex.

Many took a common narrative, i.e. the god-king-hero fights an opposing power (bad weather or natural disasters, high infant mortality, neighbouring tribe etc.); he suffers badly – sometimes he even dies; he is resurrected; and thus the myth of creation is symbolically recreated; there is a sacred marriage, a triumphal procession and finally a settling of destinies for all the characters concerned. If only life were that simple.

'Is he a friend of yours, dear?' Cave painting of hunter dressed as his prey, 15,000–10,000 BC.

3300 BC Thin, flat stones used in Egypt for grinding up malachite (used in eye painting) develop into significant works of art.

3000 BC Palaces at Knossos and Phaestos in Crete are built, possibly by settlers from Egypt, the earliest known examples of European architecture.

c.2600–2500 Funerary objects including effigies, armour and personal possessions are placed in the royal tombs of Ur.

4000~500 BC

A Horus Line

Passion in the pyramids

Set for a pyramid play.

Egypt had 'pyramid' plays, coronation festival plays, 'heb seds' (coronation jubilees) and passion plays dating back to almost 4000 BC. There were also Ra (sun god) plays about his nocturnal fight with Apophis, snake-god of the underworld: Ra always won.

The most famous passion play was the *Osiris Passion Play*, performed at Abydos between 1887 and 1849 BC. As always, this concerned the murder and dismemberment of Osiris, an early king (who subsequently became a god) by his brother Seth, and the reassembling of his body by his wife-sister (yes, that's what it says) Isis, and their son, Horus. Of course you can guess which bit they always had the most trouble finding.

The performance included battles on land and water, voyages on the Nile, and a scary resurrection scene. The action took several days to complete and audiences joined in the fighting, half supporting bad Seth, and half yelling for Horus. The actor/soldiers who slew Osiris were possibly sacrificed (thereby setting the tone for the future treatment of 'extras').

The pyramid plays were religious ceremonies with 'acted' sections about either the ascent of a deceased king's soul

PROMPT BOX

The first actor ever mentioned in recorded history was one I-kher-nefert (hence the ancient pre–performance chant of actors: 'I-kher-nefert remember me lines!'). He was also the first theatre luvvy: his account of producing a dramatic celebration of Osiris at Abydos extols his great performance as Horus, his building a boat for Osiris, the 'splendid costume' with which he bedecked an actor, ad nauseum.

c.1800 BC A taboo against eating pork appears among some peoples of the Near East; they are sheep-herding peoples and the pig is a domesticated animal of their farming enemies.

1567-1320 BC The first glassware is made; moulded glass is decorated with coloured trails, solid glass engraved and coloured rods fused to make mosaic glass.

1122 BC During the Chou dynasty, sacred rituals of worship begin to incorporate a dramatic element.

Supporting Roles

As he 'killed' the demon Apophis, a priest would chant: 'I have cut his vertebrae at the neck... I have made him non-existent; his name is not; his children are not; he is not and his family is not; his false-door is not; his heirs are not. His egg shall not last, nor shall his seed be knit together.' Now that is what I call Final.

to become one of the Imperishable Stars, or his resurrection (or, if he was seriously popular, both). The main characters were, once again, Osiris and Horus. Osiris would have represented the dead king and Horus the living one (this role was sometimes played by the new king himself).

The resurrection of the dead king was the centrepiece of the whole action and would have called for a physical presence to rise from the grave. When a priest intoned to the corpse of Osiris, 'Your Highness! Cast off the bricks – the sand – the wrappings that bind you!' it was a situation *screaming out* for a 'body' to rise up spookily. Only a senior priest could have that role (and, no doubt, the most outrageous costume Wardrobe could find).

Horus being a hero. Before the advent of animatronics they used real hippos.

Behind the Scenes

There was some sort of stage machinery evident in these texts – usually in the form of boats and carriages to carry Osiris and Horus. Elaborate masks, both for the deities and other, animal, figures were made. Their supporting shoulder straps can be seen in contemporary hieroglyphics.

The coronation plays celebrated the accession to power of a new Pharaoh, and each separate 'scene' was acted out at various points along the route of a procession. A papyrus manuscript of one example of this kind of drama was found in a worm-eaten state by the Pharaoh Shabaka around 800 BC. He had it carefully copied on to a stone slab for his father. This stone still exists, though it has proved difficult to read since in more modern times subsequent generations of Egyptians have used it as a millstone (which is just what the West has done with Shakespeare's scripts!).

'You've overdone the green again, girls.' Osiris gets his makeup done in the trailer by the goddesses Isis and Nephthys. From the *Book of the Dead*.

1000-500 BC Mycenaean pottery is painted in geometric patterns, in particular the 'key' pattern.

600 BC the roman forum ceases to be used as a cemetery.

570 BC The Greek philosopher Anaximander, considered to be the founder of astronomy, is also credited with producing the first map.

1200~500 BC

Tragedy, Comedy and Haemorrhoids

The famous Greeks

Although there is evidence of Greek drama in Syria from about 1200 BC, most of what we think of as classical Greek theatre was produced in the 5th century BC. Their word theatron *('watching space') gave us the name 'theatre'. The earliest dramas took place at the five- or six-day festivals in honour of the god Dionysus (seems like a good idea). The first theatre buildings were wooden, but later semi-circular ones were built of stone utilizing natural hollows in hillsides.*

Three Unities

Aristotle, though not a dramatist, laid down the basic do's and don'ts of classical tragedy in his *Poetics* (around 330 BC.). In particular, all drama was to observe the Three Unities (not a Motown girl group) of time, place and action, although he only goes on to explain what the unity of Action was, not the other two. Nevertheless, this stuff influenced the theatre's development until at least the 17th century.

The most notable ruins are at Epidaurus, Thoricus and the Theatre of Dionysus at Athens, where the works of AESCHYLUS (?525–456 BC), SOPHOCLES (?496–406 BC) and EURIPIDES (?480–406 BC) were performed. They seated around 14,000 people – about half the population of Athens – and, whereas some accounts say women weren't allowed in, others suggest the heady mix of tragedies, comedies, satyr plays, flowing wine and all those phalluses was so overwhelming that men fainted and women had miscarriages. The plays were also very long and, although there is no actual record of haemorrhoids, we all know what sitting on a stone seat for long periods can do.

Basically, classical Greek drama fell into three forms: tragedy, satyr and comedy. Tragedy wrestled with the big political

PROMPT BOX

The existing Theatre of Dionysus, mentioned above, is actually of Roman build (to Greek design with Roman additions up to A.D. 61). There are only five pieces of rock on the site which are confirmed to be from 5th-century Greece.

534 BC Pisistratus, tyrant of Athens, introduces a contest in Tragedy as part of the festival of 'The Great Dionysia'.

524 BC Siddhartha Gautama abandons asceticism; sitting under the famous Bo tree at Benares, he has a vision of what he must teach. In time he will become the Buddha.

300 BC Roman hairdressers are familiar with the art of hair-tinting and can bleach hair with Savon de Hesse.

Protruding Appendages

Piety apart, since the whole affair was in honour of Dionysus, the God of Wine and Bonking, all texts were basically about sex. Note, the word tragedy comes from *tragos* (goat) and *ode* (song) – satyrs were naked half animals who did naughty things to women (and each other), and most characters wore phalluses.

issues (life, death, the gods, will-the-sky-fall-on-our-heads?), the satyr (half man, half animal – usually goat) poked fun at them, whilst the comedy laughed at everyday life. The first known producer/director was Thespis (hence 'thespian'), who, it is said, 'invented' the actor around 550 BC when in one of his 'productions' he had someone step forward and answer the chorus – thus creating stage dialogue. The next great writers were Aeschylus, Sophocles and Euripides, who wrote tragedies and satyr plays, and Aristophanes (?448–?380 BC) and Menander (?160–?120 BC), who wrote comedies. The Dionysian festival plays took the form of a competition between local poets who would present three tragedies and a satyr play which dealt with a single myth or subject. This play grouping was known as a tetralogy, and the *Oresteia*, written by Aeschylus in 458 BC, is one of the best examples. Sophocles' *Oedipus Tyrannus* (c. 430 BC), although not as widely known, features one of the most famous, if least understood, characters in theatre (and later psychoanalytic) history – that geezer who loved his mother.

A couple of thespians staggering along the morning after their first-night party.

Behind the Scenes

The Greek theatre developed the orchestra ('dancing space'): a level, circular, earth-floored area in front of the rectangular stage which had dressing areas to each side. The stage roof was used for acting, too – probably for the entrance of any gods (e.g. *deus ex machina* – 'god out of the machine'). There was also a crane (*mechane*) for 'flying' actors and a platform on wheels (*ekkyklema*) for showing gory tableaux scenes.

Sometimes the mixture of searing heat, stone seats, violent deaths and Dionysian excess was too much for some of the participants.

283 BC The great Alexandrian lighthouse – one of the Seven Wonders of the World – is built on Pharos.

63 BC Mithridates VI of Pontus, having used poison homeopathically as an antidote against assassination, has to be helped to commit suicide by a Gaulish servant.

364 BC The first known raised stage is erected in Rome; the first permanent stone theatre will be built in 55 BC.

250 BC ~AD 500

'Never Work with Animals...'

Rome and panto

Whatever you've heard about the Romans, it was probably all true. Yes, they had a theatre, but it was entirely lifted from the Greeks, and anyway it came a poor second to breakneck chariot races, gladiatorial fights to the death and hunting Christians with pack animals. And why not? Rome had its dramatic festivals from the 6th century BC called ludi *(meaning 'games'), but the biggest attractions tended to be rope dancing and boxing rather than more cultural pursuits.*

Simply Beastly

At the turn of the millennium, tigers, crocodiles, giraffes, bison, rhinoceroses and hippopotami were imported to fight each other (or Christians). In AD 80 the Colosseum staged 'games' lasting one hundred days, during which nine thousand animals were slaughtered. One time, bears hidden in a theatrical 'setting' of woodland and hills killed a criminal dressed as Orpheus. Where was his social worker? In the artists' bar, perhaps.

'Do you know, Tarquin, I've got a funny feeling these aren't men in animal suits after all!'

Translations of Greek farces crept into these events around 240 BC, but not a single play survives with a plot invented by a Roman. They were far more interested in the cut and thrust (literally) of show business than all that intellectual stuff. The local magistrate who organized the games would book an actor-manager (Roman invention), who had his own troupe of slaves and foreigners as performers, to create a good show. If the play was popular, the actor-manager received money or some special gift, and if it wasn't, they featured on the top of the bill – with the lions. This system inevitably produced claques of hired applauders who would manipulate audience response by cheering favoured productions and booing others (thus giving some idiot the idea of inventing an entirely redundant career suitable only for oleaginous ne'er-do-wells; that of Critic).

There was no satirical comedy for, unlike the Greeks, the Roman court was intolerant of self-mockery. Tragedy followed, based on Greek models, but comprising more blood and guts rhetoric

AD 1–500 Roman artists paint murals portraying everyday life, landscapes and genre scenes.

472 Vesuvius erupts; falls of ash are reported as far away as Constantinople.

527 The monk Dionysus Exiguus introduces the chronological notation Anno Domini, AD.

A typical matinée performance in the Colosseum, around AD 100.

of the dull-but-earnest 'For King and Country' sort than any kind of philosophical debate.

The dramatic form for which Rome is most remembered is comedy and the pantomimes. The most admired exponents of the former were *PLAUTUS* (?254–?184 BC) and *TERENCE* (?190–159 BC) (who also wrote tragedies). Both men relied entirely on Greek plots, which they Romanized and supplemented with lots of bawdy jokes and vulgarities (Plautus) or a few high-minded titters (Terence). However, it has to be said, the five-act format for tragedy created by writers like Terence and *SENECA* (?4 BC–AD 65) became the standard for Shakespeare.

The pantomime, which saw off tragedy, was a very popular grotesque dumb show performed by a masked dancer/clown accompanied by a sort of sung chorus. It is arguable there is something perpetually essential to theatre here: a robust visual, spatial and physical art form in no way subservient to literature (a mere aspect of theatre, after all). The snooty Roman upper-classes despised the pantomimes, but happily their opinions were generally disregarded. One aristocrat who loved it so much that he often performed himself was the Emperor Nero. Nuff said?

Nymphs and Shepherds

Another form favoured by both Roman and Greek courts was the pastoral drama. These were essentially lyrical poems that idealized the joys of a rural lifestyle over the corrupt urban one. To say they were rather fanciful would be churlish. After all, what's wrong with stories about nymphs and shepherds frolicking in the fields while singing about nature, duty, honour and unrequited love? Nothing at all, as far as I'm concerned.

Behind the Scenes

The Romans and the Greeks between them gave us a clear distinction between actor and audience, the control of audience by entrance fee and selection, dressing rooms and foyers. The Romans added a proper proscenium area and curtain behind which was a permanent acting/location space. Seating was covered and the whole tiered, oval *antifeatro*, holding 20,000, provided a spectacle with more actors, machines and extras than ever before or since. Like the man said, nothing succeeds like excess.

970 Hrosvitha of Gandersheim, a German nun, writes six plays based on Terence's comedies, which will be acted by her fellow nuns.

c.1000–1010 In France, the *Chanson de Roland*, an epic poem, celebrates Charlemagne and his court and the legends that had grown up around them.

1017–1050 Bernay Abbey is built, the earliest surviving Norman church.

950~1550

Here Comes the Passion Wagon

'It's all a Mystery to me... '

Around AD 470, as Rome declined, the Roman Church came down on theatre like a ton of bricks, despising the preference people showed for comedy to worship. Undoubtedly some sort of drama must have taken place, for the human spirit has always been stronger than any church. Most likely it was linked to secular festivals in winter or spring, although there are no records of dramatic activity until the liturgical texts of the 10th century (and even these would probably have been a part of the Church services).

Behind the Scenes
Both on the wagons and the fixed stages, Hell, with its gaping mouth and belching smoke, would be on the right and Heaven on the left. The central character(s) such as Adam and Eve would be hauled between the two (sounds like normal married life). The action would not be confined to the wagons either. Characters (e.g. Herod) might 'rage' all over the street if the passion took them.

Beginning with the *Quem Queritis trope* (Latin questions and answers between priest and congregation), services expanded to include a bit of acting-out from the Bible (the Slaughter of the Innocents was a good one). Eventually the Mystery and Morality plays developed outside the church (thrown out actually by Pope Innocent in 1210, Fount of Human Kindness that he was).

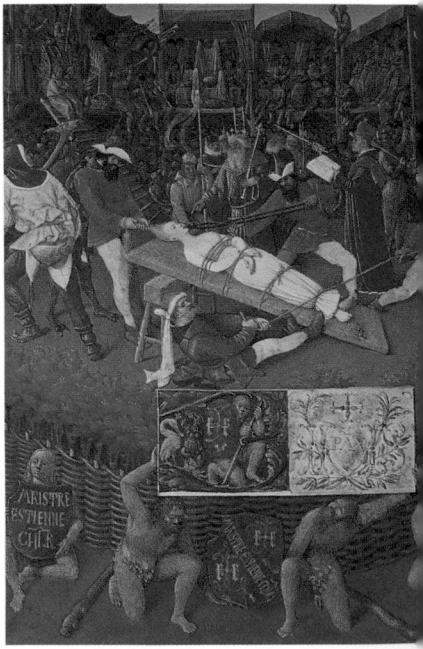

The Martyrdom of St Apollonia, one of the Miracle plays (painted by J. Fouquet). 'No, you can't call your agent. Just keep still.'

1230 An English chaplain writes a book of devotional advice for three sisters; *The Ancrene Riwle* is considered the greatest prose work of the Early Middle English period.

1373 The Dutch develop an early form of the canal lock.

1533 Ivan IV comes to power; under his rule, Russia will become a centrally administered state. He will be called Ivan the Terrible because of his reign of terror against the hereditary nobility.

During the 12th century, non-liturgical, vernacular plays based on biblical stories were performed at festivals, such as Christmas. These were called the Mystery Cycles (the 'mystery' was redemption – nothing to do with wheeled transport appearing before its time). Local lads from the crafts guilds and companies performed these 'passions' on rough wagons in procession through the streets or on fixed, circular stages. They lasted several days and, being a festival, a fair bit of drinking went on (thereby starting another thespian tradition). This theatre was probably very robust and pleasurable for all concerned, a true communal celebration of God, civic pride and creativity in the acting and making of props and costumes. And not a word of Latin was heard. This no doubt added to their undoing since it was primarily the Church, ever the killjoy, which silenced these amateur players late in the 16th century.

A Miracle play which appears to show the Devil getting dental treatment in a box theatre.

Supporting Roles

The Devil was a favourite character, both comic and frightening. His entrance was accompanied with much banging of pots and kettles, and he often rather dangerously deployed fireworks. A stage direction from The Castle *runs: 'He that shall play Baal look that he have gunpowder... in pipes in his hands, in his ears and in his arse when he go to battle.'*

The Moralities (known as 'Interludes' in their day) came later with the best known, *The Castle of Perseverance* and *Everyman*, written in the early 15th century. Moralities, though varied, had a common concern in presenting the struggle between good and evil for the soul of man. *The Castle* covered the history of mankind from birth to death. It contained the seven deadly sins, the seven virtues and the three enemies of mankind – the World, the Flesh and the Devil. *Everyman* focuses on the final moments of man when he realizes what he needs to do to gain salvation (a great deal in most cases). Above all, having a laugh was not on the agenda.

1040 Macbeth murders Duncan I of Scotland and claims the kingdom; he will rule until 1057 when he is killed in battle by Duncan's son, Malcolm.

1080 Constantine the African, a physician who he studied medicine and magic Babylon, translates Arabian Jewish and Greco-Roman medical treatises into Latin.

1133 St Bartholomew's Fair is founded in Smithfield, London; for 700 years it will be a venue for music, dancing and plays.

950~1550

Pigs' Blood, Guts and Explosions

European Mysteries

Though Mysteries on the continent developed much as did those in England, there were differences. The French were more spectacular than anyone in their sets and effects, the Spanish went in for realistic torture scenes, the Italians sang very *nicely and the Germans had their wagons in the town square long before anyone else had got up. Mostly the stories were the same with national preferences. It was the development of a wonderful sense of theatricality that separates these plays from the English ones.*

A Mystery play showing devils besieging a king. Note the proximity to the church and also to the 'Mouth of Hell'.

The most well-known French text was the anonymous *Play of Adam* (*Le Jeu d'Adam*) from the 12th century. It was a dramatized sermon, but it was notable for some very ambitious effects and varied types of characterization.

Basically it dealt with the Creation and Fall of Adam and Eve, the Cain and Abel story and a few bits and bobs from the Old Testament. At its end Adam and Eve are tied in chains by four men dressed as devils, and hauled across the stage to a smoke-belching Hell (I know people who'd pay for that). Another manuscript, of the plays performed at Valenciennes in the 16th century, describes in detail how machinery turned a 'golden ray' behind the head of God, and how the Mouth of Hell spouted fire and smoke before Lucifer rose wondrously in the air on a fiery dragon. Planned explosions, e.g. blowing up false idols 'as if of their own accord', were common too. The French

Behind the Scenes

Pageantry, a secular entertainment usually about the shenanigans of kings, developed alongside the Mysteries. Pageants involved huge processional wheeled floats of ships and castles (propelled by rows of heaving men inside), which were big enough to allow crowds of 'soldiers' to assault their decks and battlements by climbing ladders.

1307 An ordinance prohibits barber-surgeons in London from displaying blood in their shop windows for the purposes of advertisement.

1403 To prevent the spread of infectious diseases, Venice requires all travellers from the Levant to be isolated in a detention hospital for 40 days (*quaranta giorni* = quarantine).

1533 German mathematician Gemma Frisius devises a new method of surveying to replace the laborious method of pacing out distances.

The Winter Solstice, one of several traditional festivities and an important time to have a carnival for medieval folk.

also went in for endurance. A cycle at Bourges in 1536 took 40 days to complete (and 40 nights of scene changing). Some of the plays started at dawn and were 12 hours long with barely an interval (Don't you just wish you'd been there?).

Supporting Roles

Ever heard of an actor 'dying on stage'? Well sometimes... At Valenciennes, the Devil had to remove Judas' soul via his stomach (and you thought Alien *was original!) which exploded and his guts fell out (more blood in bladders). This was after he had been 'hanged' (how much would Jack Nicholson expect for this?). On occasion it really was curtains for the poor schmuck (see page 141). It's a dangerous business, this acting lark.*

In one of the Spanish Mysteries there is a stage direction to cut off a saint's breasts 'with the greatest possible cruelty'; to achieve the effect in one performance at Metz in 1468 an actor wore cardboard breasts filled with animal blood. (Pigs' blood in a bladder was a great favourite throughout Europe.) The Germans had their Mysteries and Passions – often concerned with Easter – but few Moralities. Instead they went in for the more secular entertainment of carnivals, which developed in the 15th century into the *Fastnachtsspiel* (see Herr Sachs Sucks, page 46).

Hee-haw

Ask your church to resurrect the Feast of Fools. It goes as follows:

In December the local drunk would be elected King, or Pope, of Fools for a day. There would be drinking, general indecency and a burlesque of the mass performed at its close the 'priest' would bray like a donkey and the congregation would reply 'Hee-haw, Hee-haw, Hee-haw' (I wonder why a session in parliament springs to mind?). Despite popes' and bishops' attempts to ban it, it lasted 400 years. A Jewish equivalent still exists.

1478 When Piacenza is afflicted by persistent rain, the burial of a usurer in consecrated ground is blamed; the corpse is dug up, dragged around the streets and deposited into the Po River.

1485 Henry Tudor defeats King Richard III at the Battle of Bosworth.

1492 Pope Innocent VIII, weak and in a coma, is given (probably orally) the blood of three young men, all of whom die – an early attempt at transfusion.

1470~1550

Theatre? What Theatre?

Machiavelli and the Italian Renaissance

In theatrical terms the invention of printing has a lot to answer for. Take the Italians. Before the Renaissance they were having as much fun on stage as anyone, with a thriving diversity of strong local cultures, dialects and artistic expression. Then some humanist scholars, with clearly not enough to do, discovered some Greek and Roman texts ('Ooh look lads, Classics!'). And the new-fangled printing press meant that everyone got one for Christmas.

Behind the Scenes

Movable scenery brings many new theatrical possibilities.

No one knows for sure where and when the first Italian theatre building was built. Nor is it known when they started using scenery and what it looked like. What is known is that the Renaissance marked a hugely influential change from the outdoor medieval rough stage to purpose-built indoor theatres, perspective sets, and the beginnings of changeable scenery. Playwrights sat up and took note, but did this perhaps coincide with the unionization of stage – hands?

The 'Hall of Perspective' in Rome. A likely venue for adaptations of classical plays and general camping about.

1520 Elaborate, costly scenery and costumes and fantastic interludes dominate the drama in Italy; in Spain the Inquisition quells the spirit of dramatic invention.

1521 Tribal divisions and internal strife allow Hernán Cortés to defeat the Aztec empire which extends from central Mexico to Guatemala.

1541 Michelangelo completes the *Last Judgment* in the Sistine Chapel.

First, in 1470, they printed an edition of Terence's plays and two years later those of Plautus. Then they read Aristotle's *Poetics*, which made them come over all funny, after which they would only speak in Latin! So it came to pass that the dead hand of classical imitation gripped and froze the production of 15th-century tragedies (as well as its audiences). Some wags claim their pretentious adaptations didn't even warrant the name 'theatre'. Finally, as if all this wasn't bad enough, someone thought it would be even cooler to sing the classics instead and as loudly as possible; thus was opera born.

Happily, this wasn't the case with comedies. Although these too were drawn from aforesaid Roman and Greek models, the Italian comic writers were naturally gifted at improvization and healthily cavalier about slavish translations. So the comedies developed well.

There was the commedia erudita, a literary comedy of witty banter played by amateurs to socially exclusive courts. The best of these included *Il Marescalco* (*The Stablemaster*, 1527) by *Pietro ARETINO* (1492–1556), and *La Mandragola* (1518) by *Niccolò MACHIAVELLI* (1469–1527). (Never thought of *him* writing comedies, did you?) *La Mandragola* was very much a Renaissance play, mixing classical and indigenous folk material and characters to good effect. Then there was the very famous and popular commedia dell'arte acted by professionals, to great acclaim (see pages 26–7). There was also a third branch of the comedy, even more rustic, in the work of certain dramatists who made use of local dialects and peasant character types.

The most notable actor/dramatists of this genre are Andrea Calmo and Angelo Beolco – better known as Ruzzante, a name he took from one of his characters – and it is to these truly popular theatre-makers that modern performers like Dario Fo have looked for inspiration (see page 123).

Machiavelli thinking of a screamingly funny comic plot.

School Plays

Remember the school play with horror? Well, blame the Italians; they started it! (Actually, the tradition really began in 12th-century England, but it took off in 16th-century Italy during the Reformation.) So, in the name of spiritual enlightenment and morality for young boys, Protestants staged anti-papist plays, Jesuits counter-attacked with anti-Protestant plays and both promoted anti-Semitism.

c.1500 The discovery of Greek sculpture (which had lost its colour) and Roman sculpture (which had never been coloured) influenced a move away from polychrome medieval figures.

1533 Catherine de' Medici introduces the bain marie (double boiler) to the French court; its Italian name (bagno maria) recalls the legendary alchemist, Maria de Cleofa.

1560–74 Italian writer, painter and architect Giorgio Vasari designs the Uffizi Palace in Florence, his most significant architectural work.

1500~1720

Slapstick, Dirty Old Men and Cuckolds

The Italian commedia dell'arte

The brilliant commedia dell'arte ('comedy of the profession') began in northern Italy in the mid-16th century. Its usual material was improvized comic attacks on greed, lust and status, performed on portable booth-stages that could be set up quickly indoors or out. Performers wore emblematic costumes and masks to represent stock characters. As Europe's first fully-fledged professional drama it travelled across many borders in one form or another for over 200 years.

Part of the reason it was able to do this was its vigorous visual and physical form of comedy based on traditional situations and stereotyped characters. It owed nothing to written scripting, preferring instead the 'scenario', a sort of plot summary learnt by the actors beforehand. These scenarios formed a skeletal structure on which to hang a huge variety of sketches and comic business that seemed more universal than local, and thus universally popular. Peter Brook (see page 137) would have felt right at home.

Behind the Scenes

An enduring element of the commedia was its stock characters, each with their own half masks and costumes. So, for example, a long nose and beard identified Pantalone, whilst Arlecchino wore a patched costume which eventually became the diamond pattern harlequin suit. He also carried a slapstick, two flat pieces of wood fixed at the handle which 'slapped' loudly when he used them to hit someone.

Commedia characters included on one side a group of tricksters comprising two low-status male clowns or *zanni*, the stupid but hungry Arlecchino (Harlequin) and the crafty Brighella. On the other were two old fools, a lecherous trader, Pantalone, and Il

1600 Observing two children playing with lenses in his shop leads Dutch spectacle-maker Hans Lippershey to invent the telescope.

1692 One of the last outbreaks of witch-hunting occurs in Salem, Massachusetts and 20 people are executed.

1720 After losing his provincial inheritance, Pierre Marivaux embarks on a successful career as a dramatist with *Arlequin poli par l'amour* at the Théâtre Italien in Paris.

Supporting Roles

The travelling commedia players influenced all of Europe, especially France and Spain. In fact their residencies in Paris at the Hôtel de Bourgogne were so successful the place was renamed Hôtel des Comédiens *Italiens ordinaires du Roi, and the French had to call their comedy the* Comédie Française *to distinguish it from the* Comédie Italienne. *Molière shared 14 years, from 1658, at the same theatre as the Italians.*

Dottore, a weak and pedantic academic. One of these two often had a daughter or young wife called Isabella. In addition there were two lovers (various names), a bragging soldier, Capitano, and a smart and witty serving wench, Columbine. The scenarios generally involved the tricksters trying to get their hands on the money/daughter of the old fools, and the stock-in-trade was vulgarity, bawdiness and sexual innuendo. They perfected many examples of *lazzo* (comic devices) and *burla* (practical jokes). Traditionally they spoke jargon gibberish suitable for their roles as soldier, academic or whatever. (Arlecchino spoke comic gibberish anyway.) The commedia troupes were the first to put women on the stage on equal (sometimes more favourable) terms with men. The roots of the commedia are unknown. Some have tried to link it to the Roman farces 1,500 years earlier but, although there are superficial resemblances, commedia is much more complex. A more probable antecedent is the clowning, acrobatics, patter, dancing and singing that had always been a part of popular entertainment.

Vulgarity

Sexual vulgarity has been a very basic ingredient of theatre probably from the beginning, and until the 16th century, was acceptable to both court and common society. It is found in rituals and performances all over the world to this day. For example, the Cherokee Indians, in their Bongar dance, pad their bottoms and stomachs, wear phalluses and take names like Black Buttocks, Rusty Anus and Big Testicles. (So that's where all those old heavy-metal rockers got it from).

Harlequin and Scaramouche in the hands of Roman cab drivers. A scene from the comedy *La Foire St Germain*, from 1695.

1486 Columbus persuades Ferdinand and Isabella of Spain to back his plan for a westward expedition; previous appeals to Portugal, France and England have failed.

1492 Luis de Torres and Rodrigo de Jerez report seeing natives 'drinking smoke' in the New World; Rodrigo will later be imprisoned by the Spanish Inquisition for his 'devilish habit' of smoking.

1499 Fernando de Rojas' novel in dialogue *La Celestina (Tragicomedia de Calisto y Melibea)* combines romance, everyday life, obscenity and entertainment.

1472~1650

Golden Age of Spain

Cervantes, de Vega, Calderón

An exorcism of a so-called 'bad woman'. She was probably just a bad actress, but who can blame them? Painting by Lucas y Padilla.

Spain's drama in the 16th century developed at a pace as rapid as that of its politics and fortunes. It grew out of the same medieval roots as the rest of Europe – religious yet a teensy bit profane. Spain of course had a strong Catholic Church that was never what you might call liberal-minded ('No one expects the Inquisition'). But as long as actors stayed on the right side of heresy (wave your phallus about by all means but never claim to hear voices, ok?) they were allowed to continue.

There are texts from 1472 (e.g. *A Dialogue between Love and an Old Man*, by Rodrigo Cota) written in the vernacular (i.e. not Latin). Of interest is the notorious and successful *Celestina*, also by Cota. This bold, frequently obscene and moralizing romance went through 30 editions from 1499 and was translated into French, German, Dutch, English and Italian. Unlike the Italians, Spain sensibly avoided trying to duplicate the 'classics' of Greece and Rome. Writers like Encina,

Behind the Scenes

Spain developed rectangular theatres (modelled on courtyards – as opposed to the English circular ones based on bear-baiting rings). The principal Spanish theatre in the sixteenth century was the Corral de la Cruz in Madrid. Like its English counterparts it had a three-level stage with trap doors, a gallery, balcony, rear inner stage, and was open to the elements (though with a canvas covering against the heat of the sun). Plays started in the late afternoon (after a good lunch and a bit of a siesta – how civilized!) and audiences either stood in the pit or sat in the surrounding tiers to watch the action.

1536 When Henry VIII dissolves the monasteries, England begins to suffer from a honey shortage; the monks had kept bees to provide wax for their votive candles.

1577 El Greco, born in Crete and trained in Italy, settles in Toledo; his paintings uniquely blend these three influences.

1630 Tirso de Molina's play *El Burlador de Savilla* is based on the legend of Don Juan; the story will be used subsequently by Molière, Mozart and Lord Byron.

OK Corral

A corral theatre was discovered and restored in the 1950s at Amalgro. Although its age is unknown, a pack of 17th-century cards was found in a rear dressing room (actors were obviously no more overworked then than now). This corral has three little balconies and a women's gallery (called the *cazuela*, or 'stewpan' – no comment!) because, unlike London, mixing of the sexes was considered far too licentious. Or was it that they were just terrified of women?

Torres Naharro and Gil Vicente (who was actually Portuguese) gained fame in courts with their *comedias* (plays about the nobility, clergy and their servants) and *autos sacramentales* (religious plays). Torres Naharro's works were savage and satirical about the court and the Church and consequently were banned by the Inquisition. He fled to Naples never to return.

Cervantes reading reviews of his first play. Before turning to writing he'd been captured by Barbary pirates and wounded fighting Ottoman Turks.

Miguel CERVANTES (1547–1616) (he of *Don Quixote* fame) tried his hand at dramas, but achieved little success. It wasn't until the magnificent talent of *Lope* DE VEGA (1562–1635) arrived that Spain's place on the theatrical map was assured. A direct contemporary of Shakespeare, he perfected the three-act drama where action was more important than character sketches. He is said to have written 1,500 dramas in his life (an exaggeration, surely, since only 314 are agreed to be his. Many lesser writers liked to use his credit-worthy name). Among his most famous works are *The Idiot Lady* (1613), *Madrid Spa* (1602–12) and *The Dog in the Manger* (1613–15). After de Vega came the other great Spanish Golden Age writer *Pedro* CALDERÓN DE LA BARCA (1600–81). Between 1629 and 1640 he wrote his best comedies, tragedies, historical dramas and autos including *La vida es sueño* (*Life is a Dream*, 1635) and *La cena del rey Baltasar* (*Belshazzar's Feast*, 1632).

Lope de Vega.

1547 Any able-bodied person in England who does not work may be branded with a V for Vagrant and be obliged to work as a slave for two years.

1549 The First Prayer Book of Edward VI is published; this and a second book in 1552, composed chiefly by Archbishop Cranmer, will strongly influence English prose style.

1555 Richard Chancellor and others found the Muscovy Company (the Association of Merchant Adventurers), the first of the great English trading companies, to trade with Russia.

1485~1603

Tudor Days

Ralph Roister Doister to Gorboduc

Elizabeth I loved a good masque.

From the fourteenth century virtually all of the European monarchs loved to prance about in masks and costumes whenever there wasn't a war on; goes with the job, I suppose. The Tudor kings were no different. Whenever a dignitary arrived at the court of Henry VIII, for example, theatrical Disguisings (wearing of masks and costumes) took place with the monarch at the centre of things.

Serial killers

Gorboduc had a great blood 'n' guts storyline. The younger son of a king kills his brother, whereupon his mother kills him. The people revolt and kill both king and queen. The nobles kill the rebels – and then kill each other over succession to the crown. Unfortunately, however, all action happened off-stage and was relayed only by messengers reeling off hundred-line speeches. Definitely must have been written by lawyers.

These events were amateur but lashings of money was spent on them and they were prepared with as much professionalism as any play. (Of course they were – everyone knew how Henry reacted when he was displeased!) So the Tudor court enjoyed spectacles where costume and sets were lavish, but there was no story (except their own magnificence). But in the schools and universities, where some Greek and Latin was studied (despite the Reformation during which anything Italian was Not a Good Thing), stories began to appear.

Whereas the Italians had made absurdly pompous versions of the Roman classical texts of Terence and Plautus, and the Spaniards had sensibly avoided them, one or two English writers had a go with better success, even realizing their comic

1556 Nuremberg shoemaker Hans Sachs' play *Der Paur im Egfeur* dramatizes anecdotes and everyday incidents; he will appear as a character in Wagner's *Die Meistersinger von Nürnberg*.

1559 Ice cream is made in Italy after it is discovered that ice and salt make a freezing combination.

1562 English navigator John Hawkins hijacks a Portuguese ship carrying African slaves to Brazil and makes a huge profit when he trades his human cargo at Hispaniola.

potential arguably better than had the originals. An Eton master, *Nicholas* UDALL (1504–56), penned a Roman-inspired rowdy comedy, *Ralph Roister Doister*, in 1550. Later, around 1560, a Cambridge art master, William Stevenson, wrote the more homely *Gammer Gurton's Needle*. This latter play has proved more enduring, as witnessed by various minor productions up to this century. It is written in rhymed doggerel and concerns comic gossip and upheaval in a village over the loss of Gammer Gurton's needle. Surely this essential text is due for a new revival, preferably by Steven Berkoff?

Not all plays of the time were a series of jolly japes. Four years after the coronation of that most vain, capricious, tight-fisted, wily, brilliant and nationalistic redhead, Elizabeth I, (who did so much to promote the 'Great Age' of English theatre, although not financially, I hasten to add, not a chance!), a tragedy, written after the style of Seneca, appeared. The play, *Gorboduc*, was a joint venture between two young lawyers, *Thomas* SACKVILLE (1536–1608) and Thomas Norton. It was first performed to the Queen *et al.*, and, although dull, it was in English and blank verse to boot, and was thus instrumental in establishing the five-act form for tragedy later pursued by Marlowe and Shakespeare (see pages 32–5).

Supporting Roles

The professional actor was gaining ground during the 16th century, usually under royal or noble patronage (which helped protect them against the vagaries of politics or religious prejudice). Henry VII had four players in his employ; Henry VIII doubled the number. So, by the time the great plays came along in Elizabeth's reign, there was a pool of talent ready and waiting to act them. They were still regarded as low-lifes, however. It was illegal to challenge an actor to a duel, for example, as they were not considered gentlemen. If a gentleman became an actor, he lost his gentlemanly status.

Elizabeth I on the way to the theatre. Some of her bearers have spotted an agent, and one has forgotten his tights.

1552 Italian anatomist Bartolommeo Eustachio's *Tabulae Anatomicae* describes what will be called the Eustachian tube (in the ear) and the Eustachian valve (of the heart).

1558 After 211 years of English rule, the French channel port of Calais falls to François, duc de Guise.

1563 Protestant martyrologist John Foxe's *Actes and Monuments* is published in English; popularly known as *The Book of Martyrs*, it is inaccurate, partisan, naive and vivid.

1550~1625

The Glory Days

The Burbages, Marlowe, Jonson

Christopher Marlowe, looking remarkably healthy for a chap with such a dissolute lifestyle.

The years of Elizabeth's reign saw an incredible burst of theatrical energy, interest and talent. About one in eight Londoners regularly went to watch performances of Marlowe, Shakespeare, Jonson and others, a rate only matched by cinema around 1925–39. Arguably this was the last time in England during which theatre was a truly communal activity in which audiences were respected and their aesthetics and expectations matched on stage. It has since loftily elevated itself ever further from its public.

One likely lad, a carpenter, *James Burbage* (c.1530–97) (also an actor with Lord Leicester's men), reckoned that there might be a good living in owning a purpose-built public theatre. So, in 1576, his open-air playhouse, known as the Theatre, was built at Shoreditch (outside the city walls since the Puritans weren't terribly keen on these 'chapels of Satan'). He was right, and by 1600 the Curtain, Rose, Swan, Globe and Fortune were all doing good business. His son, Richard, became one of the best, and best-known, actors of Shakespeare's great roles.

Clever Witt

If it hadn't been for the doodles of a Dutch tourist we wouldn't have much pictorial evidence of the Elizabethan stage. Johannes de Witt, a traveller visiting London in 1597, wrote in his diary about the theatres he had seen. He also made a drawing of the interior of the Swan. This was very helpful of him, as there are only three other (inferior) drawings of London theatres of the time.

Christopher Marlowe (1564–93) had a typically Elizabethan, short and violent life, dying at 29 in a pub brawl. He was also reportedly a spy, a flamboyant homosexual and an outspoken atheist

1612 English dramatist Thomas Heywood's *An Apology for Actors* is the best contemporary summary of traditional arguments defending the stage.

1614 Scottish mathematician John Napier publishes the first table of logarithms.

1630 In Japan, two families develop Kikkoman soy sauce; Kikko is the Japanese word for tortoise shell and the hexagonal pattern on tortoise shells becomes their trademark.

Masques were performed at Twelfth Night and other celebratory dates, initially in the banqueting hall of Whitehall Palace. Typical of the genre was *The Masque of Blackness* suggested by Queen Anne, who wished to appear as an African to her court! Dutifully, Jones and Jonson concocted a story about some 'daughters of the river Niger' who were travelling the world seeking a cure for their blackness in order to become beautiful! For *The Masque of Queens* (1609) Jonson added a new ingredient, an anti-masque, a grotesque or comic foil to the serious action in the drama. The intention was to provide contrast or balance to the events.

To Inigo Jones, the masque was essentially a vehicle for spectacular display. However, to Ben Jonson it was a dramatic poem based upon classical scholarship, and he often chided Jones for too much pomp and spectacle at the cost of the drama. Eventually, in 1634, they fell out irrevocably and the masque declined both in quality and in favour.

Big Spenders

The cost of some masques was amazing. Ben Jonson's *The Masque of Oberon* cost £1,500, about three times the cost of building the Fortune theatre the year before. James I, a man not known for generosity, once spent £4,000 on a single production of another masque. Today's equivalent would be about £250,000, or the cost of a 'think tank' for the English National Opera.

Worth every penny. Not.

The Last Masques

The masque declined during the reign of Charles I and both king and genre died out with the Civil War. Watching dainty courtiers mincing about in fancy dress wasn't Cromwell's most favourite entertainment (unless they were heading towards the scaffold). The last masque before the Puritans became revolting was *Salmacida Spolia* by Inigo Jones (1640). It featured a violent storm in which Fury invokes 'evil spirits to bring discord throughout England'. Do you think he knew something?

'Do you think we've overdone things a bit this time?' A masque in the *Bonner Hoftheater*.

1563 The Anglican Church is established, using dogma that is largely Protestant and a hierarchy like that of the Catholic Church.

1602 Various Dutch companies trading with Indonesia amalgamate to form the Dutch East India Company which will drive Portugal out of the spice trade within ten years.

1648 Approximately 1,000,000 black slaves have been shipped from Africa to the New World.

1550~1700

Big Noses and Bad Manners

The Renaissance in France

In 1548 the Paris Parlement banned Mystery Plays, stifling a popular voice of political protest. From being its co-originator and patron, the Catholic Church became drama's enemy. For a century French actors weren't allowed a church burial unless they renounced their profession. The Protestant Church in Germany was similarly unimpressed with theatre.

Rodrigo shows them the way to the Green Room in Corneille's *El Cid*.

There were some farces and moralities performed, but the Confrérie de la Passion (Confraternity of the Passion), who had been given a monopoly over all drama in Paris, restricted performances to their own theatre, the Hotel de Bourgogne. And when the voice of a common people is stopped, who steps in? That's right, it's those dull, academic, power-tripping minorities who never get out and have no friends. I mean the usual suspects like the Jesuits and the Humanists trying to either resurrect the language of the élite (Latin) or 'classic' dramas of the Romans. If it's old, it must be safe, right?

Fortunately, in 1570, the Italians came to the rescue in the form of visiting commedia dell'arte troupes. And one dramatist at least, *Alexandre HARDY* (1560–1631), could recognize slapstick from slipshod. His comedies breathed a little life back into the French stage. However, it wasn't until 1634 that Cardinal Richelieu ended the monopoly of the Confrérie by bringing another company to Paris to the Marais theatre.

One of the writers this company used was *Pierre CORNEILLE* (1606–84), a poet-dramatist and the creator of the brilliant

Supporting Roles

Cyrano de Bergerac was outrageous. His last play, Le Pédant joué, *at the Hôtel de Bourgogne, featured the pompous actor Montfleury as the pedagogue. Bergerac thought his performance so bad he ordered him not to act for a month. Montfleury ignored him, but the following night Bergerac returned to the theatre and drove him from the stage at swordpoint. That's what I call Criticism. Montfleury? Non, merci.*

1650 The minuet is introduced at the French Court.

1675 French courtesan Ninon de Lenclos, whose salon attracts the principal literary and political figures of her day, admits at 60 that she owes her beauty to cosmetic aid.

1693 Louis XIV sets up a committee to devise the *romains du roi* typefaces for the Imprimerie Royale; they are the first to be designed with engraving rather than calligraphy in mind.

tragi-comedy of love and revenge, *Le Cid* (1637). The leading tragedian of his day, he wrote more than 30 plays, mostly in the Neo-Classical style, including *Horace* (1640) and *Polyceute* (1643).

The principal French thespians to follow included *Cyrano* DE BERGERAC (1620–55), *Jean* RACINE (1639–99) and, of course, Molière (see pages 42–3). Bergerac was more famous for his wordplay, swordplay and long nose (all immortalized in Edmond Rostand's drama bearing his name) than for his plays.

Racine was undoubtedly a brilliant poet and tragedian, writing masterpieces such as *Andromaque* (1667), *Iphigénie* (1674) and *Phèdre* (1677). He wrote one comedy, *Les Plaideurs* (1668), but no one thinks it's very funny. By all accounts, he was also a rather nasty and ingratiating person. He wrote lyrical odes to Louis XIV (for reward) and generally pandered to the aristocracy. After the Acadèmie Français, in an act of unbelievable stupidity, refused the dying Molière an academic Chair because he wouldn't renounce acting, they offered it to Racine instead, who unhesitatingly accepted. ('All academics are jealous of artists.' Discuss.)

Controlling the Riff-raff

The Confrérie had a lot of trouble maintaining their monopoly and spent much time chasing 'illegal' actors and performers of all shapes and hues. Legitimate acrobats, rope dancers and singers who appeared at fairs and medicine shows had an unreasonable habit of bursting into bits of tragedy, comedy and farce when no one official was looking, and then running off before the authorities could say 'I arrest you!'

Rostand's play *Cyrano de Bergerac* with Antony Sher (right) in the title role as the man with the big nose.

1629 Mexico City is flooded with up to six feet of water and is described by one onlooker as resembling a shipwreck rather than a city.

1635 A mail coach between London and Edinburgh provides Britain's first inland postal service.

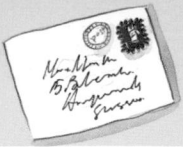

1653 Philippe Quinault is the first playwright known to have received a percentage of receipts rather than a lump sum for a production of *Les Rivales*.

1622~1673

Molière the Great

Innovative social comedy

The best dramatist France has ever produced, and one of the best in theatre history, MOLIÈRE (Jean-Baptiste Poquelin, 1622–73) was also a brilliant actor. And so loved has he been as an intrinsic part of French culture that during World War II French soldiers are known to have carried paperback editions of his works. Yet he lies in an unmarked grave. Slighted authority has a very long memory.

Molière: as great as Shakespeare and a much better actor.

Last Rights

Ironically, Molière died on stage of a coughing fit whilst playing the title role in his last play, *L'Invalide imaginaire*. The all-forgiving Church denied him the sacrament of Extreme Unction and stipulated that he be buried at night in unconsecrated ground (Jesus would probably have wept). However, thousands of his fans and friends processed by torchlight with his cortège. Did the clergy quake with fear, or just pour themselves another sherry?

Stage-struck as a boy, he eschewed careers in his father's upholstery business and in law to work with the amateur stage. His first attempts were not too successful and he ended up in a debtors' prison. He was fortunate in joining the Béjarts' company Les Enfants de Famille, led by the actor Charles Dufresne, who established precedents in small-scale theatre practice to which any modern company is forever indebted. He stayed several years with this company, writing plays, e.g. *L'Étoudi* (*The*

1654 The water for New York City comes from a well operated by hand; Tokyo has been supplied by an aqueduct since the 1640s.

1670 Pierre Puget, charged with designing a fleet of new warships, is ordered by Louis XIV's chief minister to stop making his ships beautiful.

c1672 Charles II orders that judges should wear wigs in court, as is the practice in France.

Blunderer, 1653) and *Dépit amoureux (Lovers' Quarrel*, 1656) and acting. *Le Docteur amoureux* (*The Doctor in Love*, 1658) so impressed Louis XIV he sponsored Molière from then on. In 1662, at the age of 40, he married the teenage Armande Béjart and wrote *L'École des femmes* (*The School for Wives*, 1662), a reflection on the incompatibility of youth and age and the role of women! The Church accused him of immorality and his rivals pilloried him in their own second-rate works. Molière wiped the floor with them all in *La Critique de l'École des Femmes* so thoroughly yet good-humouredly that Louis commissioned him to produce some royal entertainments and even became godfather to his first child in 1664. The following year his company at the Palais-Royal was awarded a regular salary from the crown.

However, all was not easy going. His savage attack on religious hypocrisy, *Tartuffe* (1664), was closed after its première at Versailles until a revised version was created. This was done in 1667 but the Church still got the Parlement to ban it for two years. *Dom Juan* (1665) was likewise withdrawn, probably because of the favourable portrayal of its hero as freethinking and healthily cynical. Both of these works were very successful with the public but, as any zealot will tell you, 'what do they know?'. Truth has a habit of emerging long after the zealots have disappeared, as evidenced by the fact that Molière's work is admired and performed to this day!

Behind the Scenes

Like the English Elizabethan writers, Molière created his brilliant characters and situations aided only by superb acting, emblematic costumes and personal props and dialogue designed to encourage strong movement and visual display. There was never any need for high-tech machinery and stage devices. His theatre space was indoors, lit by candles, and had a pit and 'boxes' at the side for the nobility.

A scene from *Tartuffe*: the old lecher stuffs his face. Inset: Felicity Kendal as the young ingénue in a 1991 production.

1661 Covent Garden (the former convent garden of the abbey of Westminster, confiscated with other church properties in 1534) becomes London's produce and flower market.

1663 Katherine Philips, the 'matchless Orinda', is the first woman to have a play professionally produced on the London stage.

1675 Charles II founds the Royal Observatory at Greenwich, with the aim of 'finding the longitude of places for perfecting navigation and astronomy'.

1660~1710

Decadence and Women!

Restoration Theatre

After the Stuarts reclaimed the English throne in 1660, a period of great acting and physical improvement in the theatre followed. Charles II allowed Sir William D'Avenant (1606–68) to set up the Duke of York's Company at the Salisbury Court Theatre in 1660, and Thomas Killigrew (1657–1719) to establish The King's Men at the Theatre Royal which became the first Drury Lane theatre (mention of which brings a tear to the thespian eye). These two companies were granted the monopoly by Royal Patent to be the only legitimate companies in England.

Fancy Dresses

Sumptuousness was the order of the day. It is said that the Duke of York and Earl of Oxford lent robes for plays and that Charles once lent out his coronation robes (somehow can't see Elizabeth II doing that). Pepys wrote of Charles also donating £500 for 16 scarlet robes to be made for Killigrew's production of *Catiline*. If ya got it, flaunt it!

Nell Gwyn (1650–87) looking in need of some Vitamin C. Painted by Peter Lely.

A high standard of acting was set, mainly by some of the ex-boy 'actresses' (known as 'squeaking Cleopatras') from the pre-Cromwell days who were now in their forties. In 1660, one Margaret Hughes, the first actress, clambered up on stage to play in *Othello*. Then there was that redoubtable

PROMPT BOX

Italy, Spain and France had been quite happy with women on stage for many years, but Englishmen held on to their misogyny. By 1664 there were many actresses available but Killigrew, at his Theatre Royal, mainly used them in salacious comedies. He also had girls of six or seven on stage to sing lewd songs.

1677 In Mrs Aphra Behn's comedy, *The Rover*, a man appears dressed only in 'his shirt and drawers' in an amorous scene, the equivalent of a female striptease.

1698 Jeremy Collier's *A Short View of the Immorality and Profaneness of the English Stage* attacks English playwrights and accuses them of mocking the clergy.

1710 'Plumpers', or small cork balls placed inside each cheek to fill out the hollows left by missing teeth, will be in use until the 1780s.

teenage orange seller, Nell Gwyn. Her playing of Florimel in John Dryden's *Secret Love* (1667) caused Samuel Pepys to comment interestingly that she had 'the motions and carriage... the most that I ever saw any man have'. And he wasn't the only one: Charles II liked her so much that he made her one of his mistresses. Pepys also thought Thomas Betterton 'the best actor in the world' (it's not recorded what he thought of *his* 'motions and carriage', though he *did* write that the actor Edward Kynaston was 'the loveliest lady that ever I saw'. Hmmm.).

Supporting Roles

Restoration writing was notable for its rude comedies and the boozy womanizing of its writers. George Etherege's Love in a Tub *(1664), and* She Wou'd if She Cou'd *(1668), William Wycherley's* The Country Wife *(1675) and William Congreve's* The Way of the World *(1700) are all typical comedies of (bad) manners. Thomas D'Urfey mostly wrote rude songs and jokes and probably wrote on toilet walls. If so, have these walls been preserved in ancestral homes? I think we should be told.*

Betterton's wife, Mary, was an actress, and when she quit, Cibber thought she was 'without a Rival'. Elizabeth Barry had trained with D'Avenant, who thought her acting was dull. However, an affair with John Wilmot, Earl of Rochester, did her a power of good and turned her into the greatest tragic actress of the 17th century. Anne Bracegirdle was the opposite, a great comic actress whose private life was referred to as a 'model of virtue', which I think means dull. The first professional woman writer, Aphra Behn, wrote coarser plays than the men, and penned her most notable creation, *The Rover*, in 1677.

Anne Bracegirdle in Aphra Benn's *Widow Ranter*.

Behind the Scenes

Restoration theatres, such as the Theatre Royal and the Duke's Theatre were indoors, had a proscenium, flats and backdrops, a balcony and a deep apron forestage. This forestage was used most of the time because the auditorium had only candles for light, which meant the rear stage was in semi-darkness. Easy to get lost – or worse – back there.

1484 Jacob Sprenger, Dominican Inquisitor of Cologne, and Heinrich Krömer publish *Malleus Maleficarum*, a textbook on the seeking out and punishment of witches.

1509 The anonymous German prose narrative *Fortunatus* is concerned with the search for riches, a primary preoccupation of the age.

1530 To defend the newly formed Lutheran churches from Charles V, Protestant states of the Holy Roman Empire form the League of Schmalkalden.

1450~1600

Herr Sachs Sucks

Teutonic popular theatre

These days Shrove Tuesday is marked by the odd pancake, but in 16th-century Germany, particularly Nuremberg, it was occasion for the biggest carnival of all. And at the centre of it was the Fastnachtsspiel *(carnival play).*

Springing from pre-Christian fertility rites, this knockabout theatre retained some of its communal ritual form. Instead of disengaging the audience as modern drama does, it was an integral part of the revelries involving audience and performer alike in a comic, rude and robust celebration of spring and the community. Instead of appealing to the intellect, it went straight for the guts and groin (sounds simply *marvellous*, darling). Existing totally within the framework of the carnival, it was probably perceived as little different to the other entertainments on offer. The actors stepped out from the crowd at the beginning, announced their short play (about subjects like avarice, gluttony or infidelity) and performed it (with the audience taking part). At the end, they stepped back into the crowd and got on with some serious drinking. I suppose you could call it a sort of early version of punk rock.

Smack on the Wrist

Some of the *Fastnachtsspiel* plays, especially the *Lügenmärchen* (or tall stories), had elements of social satire. They used the protective licence of Shrovetide to turn their society arse over tit, as it were, and remind the townsfolk, who suffered the more outrageous stupidity and greed of aristocracy, church and local government, that things need not always be as they are. Perhaps Sachs was in the pay of the local burghers.

The Meistersingers of Nuremberg preparing to deliver another thigh-slapping toe-tapper before the release of their latest album.

1587 Thousands of Germans suffer insanity and death after eating bread made from rye infected with the ergot fungus; ergotism is endemic in the German states.

1587 German author Johan Spies compiles his *Historia von D. Johann Fausten*; the Faust legend goes back to before 1540, but this is the first published version.

1596 English poet Sir John Harington invents the water closet but people don't take to it and still prefer their chamber pots.

A favourite stock character was Pickleherring, who typified the earthy beer-swilling German jokester. At the centre of things, he would often ridicule the local burghers who ruled the town. Occasionally Pickleherring and other country peasants were themselves the object of ridicule (they were never popular with townsfolk), and this would prompt some vigorous and untheatrical physical 'debate' in the streets!

Hans SACHS (1494–1576) attempted to 'improve' later *Fastnachtsspiel* plays. He was a cobbler turned writer (or was he a writer who turned out cobblers?), who wrote 6,000 dull middle-class moralizing dramas, all of them happily forgotten. He replaced much of the healthy smut and horseplay in the *Fastnachtsspiel* with humanism, folksiness and versions of his own Lutheran religion (I bet he was welcome in the bar). He took over a deserted church in 1550 and turned it into the first indoor German theatre building. And although his plays may have been forgotten, he wasn't. Both Goethe and Wagner celebrated his 'Germanness', the latter immortalizing him in his opera *Die Meistersinger von Nürnberg*. He was probably a nice guy who remembered his mother's birthday and was kind to lame stray dogs.

Supporting Roles

Hans Rosenplüt *and* **Hans Folz** *(both roughly 1450–1515) wrote early* Fastnachtsspiel *(known as* Revuespiel*) which consisted of characters delivering comic monologues. The* Handlungsspiel *(plot-plays) of Hans Sachs were a little more similar to today's drama. But all this fun couldn't last. The Protestant Church abolished the pre-Lent carnival whilst the Catholics developed* Schuldrama *(Latin school drama), and all people called Hans were banned from writing plays. Religion stepped in to spoil the fun, just as in France (see page 40).*

Some say the Green Man (centre), a Fastnachtsspiel character, was an early precursor of Santa.

1585 Jamaican ginger reaches Britain on a ship from the West Indies. It is the first spice from the Far East to have been grown successfully in the West, but won't be the last.

1596 Everyone is trying to solve the problem of longitude. In Spain, King Philip III offers a reward of 1,000 crowns and the Dutch parliament offers 10,000 florins.

1601 William Parry's account of Anthony Sherley's expedition to Persia contains the first mention of coffee; Sherley introduces coffee to London where it sells for £5 an ounce.

1585~1650

The Brits on Tour

Browne, Kempe and the 'Englische Komödianten'

Before the Thirty Years' War ended in 1648 the only professional actors in Germany were in touring companies, first from England, then France and Italy. The Brits had been touring Europe since about 1580, mainly to escape the plague that had closed many theatres at home.

'It's no good showing them the script – they still won't get it.' An early Brits tour.

Known as the Englische Komödianten (English Comedians), they enjoyed great prosperity and fame. One of the most important companies of Englische Komödianten was organized between 1592 and 1620 by Robert Browne, for whom Count Moritz of Hesse built a private theatre in 1605 (see what I mean? In England he'd have been lucky to get a voice-over).

They had played the Dutch and Danish courts in the late 1590s and appeared at Dresden. The famous Shakespearean clown *Will Kempe* (fl. 1600) often toured with other actors in the company of the Earl of Leicester. When in Germany, they enjoyed aristocratic patronage to the extent that many decided to stay behind (see pages 46–7 for suggestions as to why).

As a repertoire they mostly produced home-country standards like *Gammer Gurton's Needle* (see page 31), comic sketches and short biblical dramas, but they also included some mutilated clownish versions of Shakespeare and Marlowe (a tradition continued to this day at the Royal Shakespeare Company). In the early years

1613 English sculptor of tomb monuments Nicolas Stone begins work in London; he is the most accomplished English sculptor of his day.

1641 An Ordinance of the English Parliament closes down public theatres in England 'to appease and avert the wrath of God'.

1646 Charles I of England surrenders to the Scottish army at Newark; the following year the Scots will sell him to the English Parliament.

they acted in their native tongue, which would have necessitated performing in a very visual slapstick style, learning just enough Low German to get by. But later they added German actors and actresses and their shows began to be performed in the German language. However the repertoire remained the same, which meant that German translations and new plays followed the same chopped up 'classic' texts and thus reproduced the same degree of coarseness, humour and violence.

Catholic Values

The most continuous theatre tradition in Germany at this time was actually in the Jesuit colleges, mainly in Bavaria and Austria. Initial plays were in Latin (gradually replaced by vernacular) and intended to educate the boys in rhetoric and Catholic values. Performances favoured spectacle and great musical scores, and may be seen as forerunners of the later spectacular operas of Germany and Bavaria. So that's where all the repression, guilt, and inhumanity comes from.

Supporting Roles

Of the few Germans who attempted to write a bit of quality for the stage, **Jacob Ayrer, Andreas Gryphius** *and* **Caspar von Lohenstein** *stand out. Ayrer wrote in the 16th century and none of his work has survived. Gryphius and von Lohenstein wrote 17th-century classical and baroque plays respectively. However, their impact was minimal since there weren't the companies to perform them. (A bit like the plight of the modern classical composer, then. One assumes they had day jobs.)*

The result was the *Haupt und Staatsaktionen*, German episodic texts, which mixed together copies of the English efforts with those of visiting Italian commedia dell'arte troupes. These plays seem to have relied on bombastic acting, gross obscenity and lots of gore splashing around the stage. Sounds like good old thigh-slapping, Teutonic fun.

Tour de France

After the Thirty Years' War ended in 1648, French companies and commedia troupes from Italy visited Germany in droves. However, whereas the commedia plays went down well – Harlequin was a particular favourite – the plays of Corneille and Racine, and even those of Molière, made no impression. Germans were still happy to watch the slapstick antics of Pickleherring (what a funny chap he must have been).

Peter Brook's *Midsummer Night's Dream* in the 1970s – all lycra and platforms.

1592 Possibly the earliest written record of a modern wig appears in the record of Henry VIII's privy purse expenses; 20 shillings 'for a peryuke for Sexton, the king's fool'.

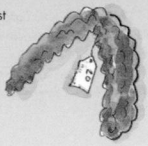

1600 Italian philosopher Giordano Bruno, condemned by the Inquisition for heresy, immoral conduct, and blasphemy, is burned at the stake.

c1650 Giovanni Bernini creates his masterpiece, *The Ecstasy of St. Teresa*, for the Cornaro chapel Santa Maria della Vittoria.

1590~1700

Baroque? Actors are Always Baroque!

Italian melodramma in perspective

If the commedia dell'arte represented one half of a culturally divided Italian society, then the melodramma (drama with music) and the scenic achievements accompanying it represented the other half. The origins of this form – which later came to be called opera – are confusing (just like opera itself).

It is thought that the activities of the *camerate* (private clubs for scholars) formed after the Restoration, with their dramas of music and visual spectacle, together with the influence of the pastoral dramas (those idyllic 'Shepherd Luvs Nymph Forever' poems of the Romans) had something to do with it. At any rate we might say both the melodramma and the commedia dell'arte are the greatest contributions Italy has made to the world stage. But only if we wanted to be rude.

Baroque theatre is essentially about mindboggling scenery and expensive sets (they had to distract attention from the weak scripts). Stage machinery was developed to feed the aristocratic taste for novelty. Clouds and whole

Family Ties

Commedia troupes liked to keep it in the family (a common Italian tendency). There were the Martinellis (Drusiano Martinelli was the first Arlecchino to visit England in 1577; his wife, Angelica Alberghini ran the Uniti), and the Biancolellis; Francesco and Isabella, and their son, Guiseppe Domenico. Giovan Andreini came from another 'family'; his parents, Francesco and Isabella, formed the Gelosi company before the Fedeli and... . I hope you're taking notes.

Italian actors struggling to hang on to an audience who expected a more inspiring set.

English diarist Samuel Pepys notes the popularity of masks for ladies of fashion at the theatre; 'and so to the exchanges to buy a vizard for my wife'.

1670 Minute hands appear on watches for the first time.

1698 French cellarer Dom Perignon pioneers the development of sparkling champagne, decanting his wine made from a new blend of grapes into corked bottles of stout English glass.

Supporting Roles

Other commedia troupes of note were the **Acessi**, *the* **Confidenti** *and the* **Compaglia degli Uniti**. *The Acessi merged with the* **Fedeli** *and the Confidenti with the* **Uniti**. *All except the Uniti (problems of budget management, mayhap?) travelled abroad and all had ceased activities by the mid-1600s. However, commedia continued in less organized forms for another hundred years, and still influences Western theatre. Old habits die hard.*

Arlequino in full flight.

groups of 'celestial' performers zoomed about on flying apparatuses, while sliding wing flats and shutters, painted with perspective-based designs, were fixed on to wheels to allow rapid scene changes. Special effects blossomed: birds sang, dragons breathed fire, cannons roared, chariots and ships crossed the stage, storms raged at sea and cities burned. Practitioners like Alfonso Parigi (who *so* impressed Inigo Jones), Giovanni Aleotti, Giacomo Torelli and Nicola Sabbatini dominated theatre design throughout Europe. Torelli, in particular, is credited with the development of a system of wheels and rollers that allowed a single stagehand to move a whole range of flats and shutters at the same time.

There was also some tragic drama written in Italy during the 17th century, but fortunately very little. Probably just one writer emerged of any consequence – actor, company manager and playwright *Giovan Battista* ANDREINI (1576/9–1654). Andreini made his name with *La Centaura*, 1622, and *Le Due Commedie in Commedia* (*Two plays Within a Play*), 1623, which have occasionally been revived. Andreini was leader of the Fedeli ('the Faithful') troupe of commedia dell'arte players. Under the patronage of the Duke of Mantua, the Fedeli created exotic court extravaganzas and travelled to the Hotel de Bourgogne in Paris in 1614. Such exorbitance and splendour... it's enough to give you the screaming vapours.

Behind the Scenes

Sabbatini left two volumes on theatre design collectively titled *The Practice of Making Scenes and Machines*, 1637 and 1638. These were full of tips for stage technicians – not useful ones like 'How to make your teabreak last two hours', but instructions on common requirements like 'How to make dolphins and other sea monsters appear to spout water while swimming', and 'How to divide the sky into sections'.

Mezzetino receiving advice from his horse.

c400-500 The complex movements and expressions of Indian dance are integral to the drama of the period.

500-600 Paintings reveal evidence of expertise in Indian textile-making, including pattern-weaving, and tie-dyeing.

1000 Theatre in India after the M invasion, as the Mos are opposed to drama

?320~1920

It's an *Epic* – So Go to the Lav First!

India: Kalidasa, Shri-Harshadeva to Tagore

A scene from the *Ramayana*: 'Wear this and your skin should return to normal.'

Whereas in the West rituals and myths informed the development of theatre, in India such rituals actually became the theatre. From a time long before Christ, Indian drama followed three pathways: Sanskrit drama, which existed up to about AD *1000, folk drama and dance drama.*

Sanskrit drama is first referred to in the pre-Christian epic period, in those great (and *very*, *very* long) poems that detail all Indian culture, history and religious beliefs, the *Mahabharata* and the *Ramayana*. The first dramatist was Bharata (*bharata* is now used to mean 'actor'), though there are few details about him. He is said to have written the *Natyasastra*, a book laying out the form the drama was to take (Rule 1: It Shall Be Very Long). However, the most creative time was the Classic period, from about AD 100 to 800. Its two principal writers were Kalidasa and a king called Shudraka. Kalidasa created *Shakuntala* (*The Fatal Ring*) much admired by Goethe (mind you, he liked Pickleherring). Shudraka is credited with *The Little Clay Cart*, a story

PROMPT BOX

Dance drama was a silent form of speech, with actors' gestures and entire bodies 'speaking' to an audience who, moreover, knew what they were saying. This theatre has influenced Western visionaries like Brecht, Artaud, Brook and Grotowski. All the really major dudes, in fact, except perhaps Beckett (imagine *Krapp's Last Tape* as a silent, solo dance).

1526 Persianized Turkish invaders conquer the Delhi Sultanate and found the Mughal dynasty which will rule most of India for over 200 years.

1877 Queen Victoria becomes the Empress of India with an ornate ceremony held in Delhi.

1917 Rabindranath Tagore has Manipuri dancing taught at his school; the dance dramas Tagore writes for his pupils will help to overcome prejudice against Indian classical dancing.

Behind the Scenes

Bharata even dictated the staging of plays. Some were to be square, some oblong, and some even triangular. These theatres had a rear stage and a thrust apron with wings for actors' entrances. No one had to stand (unlike in the Globe etc.) and seats were on a sloping platform 'like a series of steps'. There is mention of props and 'machines' but no scenery.

about a poor merchant and a rich courtesan. Another king/writer, Shri-Harshadeva, reigned in the north between AD 607 and 647, and wrote *Ratnavali* (*The Pearl Necklace*), most notable for having a parrot as the central character (a tradition more recently revived by Monty Python).

The folk drama was a kind of popular play of improvisation, with characters and themes borrowed from the 'classics'. Any texts to survive are anonymous and research suggests they varied from performance to performance. In Indian dance drama the storyline was an integral part of the experience, unlike Western dance where it's all about how high you can leap in tights and silly dresses. One dance drama form, Kathakali from Kerala, has gained an international reputation right up to today. It has an unrestrained, bold, foot-stomping style with 'superhuman' characterizations (the same guys who pop up in Bollywood cinema) and blende dance, acting and music. Unfortunately, not much of substance has survived from about AD 800 through to the works of Sir *Rabindranath TAGORE* (1861–1941), who wrote 'eastern symbolist' and Neo-Romanticist plays such as *The King of the Dark Chamber*, 1914, and *The Cycle of Spring*, 1917.

Supporting Roles

Bhasa (4th or 5th century BC) has left 13 plays of which The Vision of Vasavadatta *is amongst the best Sanskrit plays. Another writer, Bhavabuti (late 7th century), was known by his friends as 'The Sweet Speaking' (oh really?). He penned the melodramatic* Malatimadhava *(or* The Stolen Marriage*), a Romeo-and-Juliet-alike except that the lovers get a happy ending.*

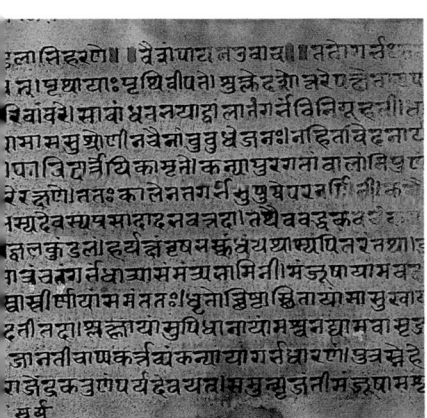

An Indian miniature based on the *Mahabarata*, the epic drama that chronicles the struggle between two rural families and the birth of the Indian nation.

1191 Tendai monk Eisai attempts to restore pure Buddhism to Japan. Through his teachings, Zen will influence martial arts, Nō plays, poetry, flower arrangement and the tea ceremony.

c1400-1500 Lakon drama-dances are imported from Cambodia into Thailand; they are based on stories from a variety of sources and danced by women.

1641 The Dutch capture Malacca from the Portuguese; the Dutch East India Company gains effective political control over the Malay archipelago.

800~today

Wajang Gedog and the Shadows!

South-east Asia: marionettes and humans

Javanese dance drama.

Several theatrical forms have flourished in South-east Asia, the most prominent being the shadow play, the puppet play and the dance drama. Stories are mythological, telling of the heroic battles of gods and kings against evil. In Burma a drama rather like that of India, and based on the Ramayana, *has been recorded since the mid-18th century.*

There were also the *Nat-pwes* (god festivals), religious occasions where female mediums 'acted out' the lives and decisions of dead gods (*nats*); these are performed in outside enclosures, with invited dignitaries sitting on platforms. (Good thing the Spanish Inquisition didn't know about *them*!) The main audience fills the enclosure and the stage is a series of mats. An orchestra is used, as are masks. Throughout Malaya and Thailand the shadow play and marionette performances have always been extremely popular.

Perhaps the most developed theatre is in Indonesia, especially Java and Bali. Javanese theatre falls into three basic forms: *wajang kulit* (shadow plays), *wajang topeng* (actors wearing masks and imitating puppets) and *wajang gedog* (pantomimic actors/dancers); *wajang* means 'performance'. The shadow plays are traceable back at

Behind the Scenes

Audiences at shadow plays sit on both sides of the screen so some will see puppets and some will see the shadows they make. All the while, the gamelan plays its drums and gongs. These plays last throughout the night because it is thought any 'malignant spirits' will have disappeared by dawn (if not, I find a glass of liver salts often does the trick).

1883 A volcanic eruption virtually destroys the island of Krakatau. Over 5,000 people die and the subsequent tidal wave kills more than 31,000 people in nearby Java and Sumatra.

1953 New Zealand climber Edmund Hillary and his Sherpa guide make the first successful ascent of Mount Everest, the world's highest peak.

1959 Tibet's Dalai Lama requests asylum in India after an unsuccessful rising against the Chinese garrison at Lhasa.

least as far as the 7th century. In these performances, the grotesque, translucent leather puppets are manipulated behind a backlit white cloth by an invisible *dalang* (leader) who recites the performance, usually learnt by heart. He moves the puppets by wooden rods attached to their thin arms (we stick our hands up the puppets' rear end; therein lies a Big Cultural Difference). He also directs the *gamelan*, or orchestra, who sit to the side of the performance space.

In the *wajang topeng* performances, dancing actors hold masks to their faces by gripping a leather piece fixed inside the mask. This means they cannot speak, so, to avoid the 'gottle o' gear' syndrome, their lines are chanted by another. This performance style is traceable to the 11th century and generally is based on Javanese versions of the *Ramayana* and *Mahabharata* with additions in the Middle Ages of a new Javanese cycle of adventures known as *Panji*.

An Indonesian puppeteer: now you know why they are traditionally kept hidden from view.

Rod puppets of the Sage Begawan Bisma and an (unhappy) maid, 19th century.

The *wajang gedog* actors perform without masks and in a pantomimic style. Initially this was a dance dumb show but Western influence has added speech. This new form is called the *wajang orang*. Plots are often melodramatic and concern the activities of hero figures, as in 'How Petruk Becomes King of Madura'. Like the other forms, these plays are performed in a building called a *pendoppo*, which is open on two sides.

Trance Dance

A Balinese speciality is the barong dance drama, usually known by tourists as the 'trance dance'. Performers pretend to be caught between two forces – the evil witch Rangda, and the good lion, the Barong, who tries to protect them (no, they don't go through a wardrobe first). It culminates in a frenzied trance during which performers roll round the floor trying to impale themselves on daggers – adding a literal dimension to the old theatrical expression, 'We died out there tonight!'

200 BC Stone chimes are among musical instruments used in China.

140 BC Caravans begin to carry 'Chinese fruit' (apricots and peaches) to Europe, and grapes, pomegranates, and walnuts are introduced to China.

444 The wheelbarrow is invented by the Chinese; during the period of the Six Dynasties they will also develop kites.

200BC~1850

Does Anyone Know What's Happening?

Things change slowly in Chinese theatre

Let's put your mind at rest... just in case you were worried. Basically the Chinese theatre has a form and tradition utterly incomprehensible to anyone in the West, so if that includes you, it's not your fault and you needn't be unduly embarrassed. Feel better now?

From *The Sun and Moon*. They haven't worked out whose turn it is to shine.

PROMPT BOX

Kublai-Khan, the Mongol Emperor, put a stop to intellectual Chinese writers getting cushy government jobs by 'persuading' them (I don't think he was a man to refuse) to divert their creative energies to something more useful and, since he liked theatre, they wrote plays, and lo! new stories of contemporary folk did gradually appear.

Though a religious drama existed during the Hsia, Chou and Tsin Dynasties (2000–200 BC), when actors were considered amongst the lowest life-forms (when are they not?), the formal beginnings of Chinese theatre were during the Tang Dynasty (AD 720–907) when puppet shows and music dramas flourished under the enlightened Emperor Ming Huang.

550 In this century the Chinese invent gunpowder, which they use in fireworks.

1230 Chen Ssu-tao writes the earliest known treatise on crickets, which are kept by the Chinese for their chirping.

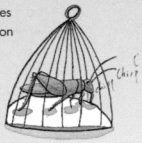

1311 Paper money, in use by the Chinese since 1236, is discontinued when treasury reserves fail to keep up with the flood of currency.

He began a school for actors in his pear garden (actors are still called Pear Tree Garden Actors). Theatre changed little in real terms from then to the 19th century, when Western influence entered the country. During the Song Dynasty (AD 960-1127) fully developed theatres, or *goulan*, appeared, the largest of which could hold thousands. Then, after the Mongols dropped by in 1234 to set up their Yuan Dynasty, the first great age of Chinese theatre began.

The mask (later make-up) and costume we associate with Chinese theatre dates roughly from this time. The main characters were the male, female, villain and clown (the usual suspects). Make-up and costume are heavily symbolic, thus a white face means wickedness, a blue face means ferocious, a red face means courageous, a black veil means the actor is playing the dead ancestor of the hero and a green face means the actor had a bad take-away the night before.

The first permanent playhouses were called 'tea houses' and had a roofed thrust stage and balconies. The audience sat on three sides chatting, eating, drinking, playing games and coming and going throughout the performance. You paid for the tea but the show was free.

The training of Chinese actors was famous (and very hard!). From childhood they would learn every single gesture in a character's 'repertoire' for up to 200 fixed roles. From the start, women were trained just as the men were. This only stopped in the 18th century when, it is said, they got smart and began to marry nobility. This remained largely unchanged until the Cultural Revolution in 1949, after which it got politically correct and boring.

Crime Minister

Confucius, he say: *'Man with big mouth not live long'.*

One emperor loved heroic dramas that paid due reverence to his ancestors. Occasionally in need of a laugh, however, he would employ dwarfs and others to perform short comic pieces in which mild criticism of him and his court was encouraged. However, if the hapless actors criticized too much, Confucius (550–478 BC), in his role as Minister of Crime, had them executed. One of the situations, perhaps, where forgetting some of your lines might be the very best thing.

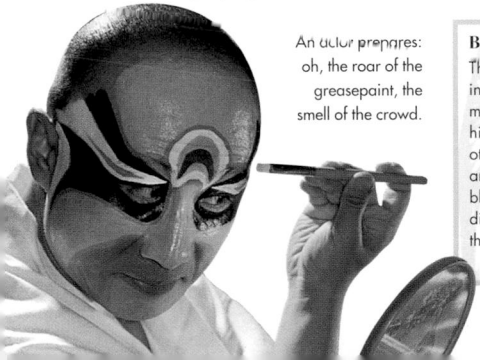

An actor prepares: oh, the roar of the greasepaint, the smell of the crowd.

Behind the Scenes

The Chinese stage has no scenery. Everything is implicit in the costume and gesture of the actor. For example, he mounts an imaginary horse by an exaggerated swiftly of his leg,and holds a wide sleeve between him and the other actors to disappear. The prop men who pile chairs and tables to symbolize a temple or boat etc. wear black to indicate they are invisible (like funeral directors). Oh, and its always useful to know these things in advance.

1300-1400 The aristocratic *nō* theatre generates a new school of Japanese decorative textiles; the bold patterns of *nō* costumes represent a departure from Chinese textile design.

1597 The warrior class in Japan represents eight per cent of the population; in contemporary Europe it is no more that one per cent.

1637 The Japanese, 'blow their Noses with a certaine sofft and tough kind of paper... which, having used, they Fling away as a Fillthy thing'.

1200~the present

No, No, Not No... *Nō!*

Monkey music and Mannerism in Japan

The Japanese theatre must be the only place in the world where an actor dreams of being called shite *(which means 'first actor' in a* nō *drama) or, failing that, just* waki *(second actor). But enough of praise. This is also one of the few theatres still performing in a style that has remained largely unchanged for seven or eight hundred years. The aristocratic* nō *dramas reflect the Japanese tendency towards austerity of style and restrained neat minimalist decorum – and once you're perfect, why bother to change it?*

Theatre came to Japan from China via Korea around the end of the 6th century. The earliest performances were the pantomimic religious dances called *Kagura*, connected to Shinto worship. Japanese theatre, like so much Asian theatre, is inextricably linked to the religious and cultural make-up of the country. It is filled with dialogue, song, music and dance and not pigeon-holed, as it is in the West (with the exception of musicals and opera) into spoken word, music or ballet, and so on.

Behind the Scenes
In addition to the stage, *kabuki* theatre has the 'flower way' – a walkway leading from the side of the stage to the back of the auditorium used for dramatic scenes. The revolving stage (an 18th-century Japanese invention) has trap doors, as does the 'flower way', to allow actors to spring startlingly into view.

The *nō* ('art/skill') theatre, with its comic sidekick *kyō gen* ('mad speech') theatre came into existence some time in

The Japanese actor in stylized pose, costume and lighting. Scary stuff! Solemn dances suggest the character's deepest emotions; in this case, disdain?

c1740 Limited colour printing for the popular Ukiyo-E prints is introduced; previously prints were blocked and then hand-coloured.

1798 London hatter John Hetherington makes the first top hat of silk shag, or plush, reducing demand for American beaver pelts.

1953 When shellfish are polluted by methyl mercury, people in the Minamata Bay area of Japan suffer from worrying symptoms, sometimes followed by derangement and death.

the 12th century, patronized by the samurai classes and spiritually enriched by Zen Buddhism. *Nō* is a highly mannered form in which actors wear masks and move to music. The *kyō gen* were conceived as necessary parts of the theatre structure (i.e. five *nō* need three *kyō gen* to stop everyone getting too depressed). The most famous

PROMPT BOX

In full flow *kabuki* actors might whip off their costume to reveal another one underneath, burst into dance, or do some pantomime business which has nothing to do with the main plot. A Japanese critic wrote: 'One might just as well climb a tree in quest of a fish as to expect logic and rationality in a *kabuki* play.' Ah so!

'I may have a smile on my face, but this is *nō* laughing matter.'

writer/performers of *nō* were *Kwanami* KIYOTSUGU (1333–84), and his son *Seami* MOTOKIYO (1363–1444). Seami developed the *sarrugaku* (monkey music – you know, three guitars and a drum kit), and was revered as the greatest *nō* performer.

Kabuki, however, was the punk rock of the 17th century. Started by a woman, O-Kuni, who went round soliciting funds for temples, *kabuki* filled the entertainment gap left by the aristocratic *nō* . With its rigid-faced, colourful actors moving like puppets, its scenery, wigs, and loads of costumes (a new one for each entrance), it proved very popular.

Bunraku

The puppet theatre known as *bunraku* grew up around the same time as *kabuki* and continues today. Life-like puppets with moving fingers, eyes and mouth, manipulated by visible puppeteers, enact emotional stories that usually end in a ritual disembowelling or decapitation of a close relative.

1708 Jean-François Regnard's play *Le Legataire Universel* has a valet as its central character, foreshadowing Beaumarchais' Figaro.

1728 French dentist Pierre Fronchard makes false teeth using gold plate with teeth of jewellers' enamel.

1765 Paris tavernkeeper Boulanger challenges the monopoly of the traiteurs and wins the right to serve a *restorante* (restorative) soup; the history of the restaurant starts here.

1700~1830

Theatre, Revolution and Short Dictators

18th-century France: Voltaire, Beaumarchais, Talma and Napoleon

In all fairness to the French, Molière and Corneille were hard acts to follow. But that doesn't entirely excuse the rubbish passing off as theatre during the 18th century. VOLTAIRE (François-Marie Arouet, 1694–1778) left off his dreary poems to have a go, but all he could manage were a few 'classical' dull-but-worthy plays.

To make things worse, two new theatre forms emerged which we could have done without: the lachrymose comedy and the bourgeois drama. The first were weepies, full of sentimental 'hero-and-heroine-suffer-dreadfully-but-all-ends-well' sort of drivel. The second, initiated by Voltaire and *Denis DIDEROT* (1713–84), were middle-class dramas – sagas of everyday life (just what theatre's best at, I don't think), serious in tone but with nauseatingly happy endings and moral lessons to be learned.

It wasn't until *BEAUMARCHAIS* (*Pierre-Augustin Caron*, 1732–99) appeared that Molière could stop spinning in his grave. This ex-watchmaker, secret agent and gun-runner was undeniably a comic genius. His best known plays, *The Barber of Seville* (1775) and *The Marriage of Figaro* (1778), later turned into operas by Rossini and Mozart, were subversive in attacking the sacred cows of aristocratic society. In this he foresaw the Revolution, so both the plays and Beaumarchais were okay. Napoleon later called *The Marriage of Figaro* a 'revolution already in action'.

Voltaire dictating to his secretary while getting dressed. He must have had an important deadline to meet. Painting by Jean Huber.

1784 Benjamin Franklin advises the French to set their clocks ahead one hour in spring and back one hour in autumn to take advantage of daylight.

1806 Jean F. Chalgrin designs the Arc de Triomphe in Paris.

1815 Allied soldiers passing through Epernay 'liberate' 6,000 bottles of champagne from the cellars of a M. Moët; the following year they will order – and pay for – the same quantity.

From *The Barber of Seville*.
'Does Sir want a little something for the weekend?'

However, it has to be said that 18th-century French theatre did produce some great actors/actresses. Adrienne Lecouvrer was by far the best actress at the Comédie Française, turning the most embarrassingly lurid dialogue into an intelligent, emotional tour de force (honest, she did; I was there...). After her came Rachel, a young sensation who enticed Molière's best actor, Michel Baron, out of retirement at the age of 67. (He quit the stage at the height of his powers and no one seems to know why. They might reflect on the lines he had to utter.) Then, in 1743, Hippolyte Clairon demonstrated an amazing degree of control and ability to portray emotion without feeling it (yes, dear, it's called *acting*). Finally, the great François Talma shocked pompous Paris in his debut at the Comédie Française in 1787 dressed in a Roman toga with bare arms (cheeky!).

In 1791, with support from Napoleon (who must have been taller than him), Talma opened the Théâtre de la République. Dictators are never too reliable, however, and 1804 saw Napoleon, who was never noted for his sense of proportion, introduce censorship (on reflection, maybe he knew what he was doing). Whereupon French theatre fell into a hole for a few years.

Party Poopers

For someone who wrote crap plays, Diderot at least knew what the experience of theatre should be about. In 1758 he attacked the posting of guards in French theatres because of 'rowdiness' in the pit. 'Before', he lamented, 'people arrived heatedly (and) went away in a state of drunkenness... to brothels (or) polite society'. 'Now' the killjoys had made 'theatres more peaceful and more respectful than churches'. He wasn't at all keen on the Church, and the attacks continued in his most important work, the influential *Encyclopédie*.

Behind the Scenes

The Revolution allowed any citizen to open up a theatre for any type of drama. It also encouraged open-air festivals such as those organized by the painter, Jacques-Louis David. A new audience, keen for spectacle, emerged. These crowds were part of the spectacle, not just observers. One of their favourite entertainments was the circus. Thus did the Franconi brothers prosper, opening their Cirque Olympique in 1807. Another highly popular spectacle of the period involved the decapitation of selected members of the aristocracy.

1704 Antonio Vivaldi is established as a teacher at the Conservatorio dell'Ospedale della Pietà in Venice and will remain there until 1740.

1718 A four-year war between Venice and Constantinople ends with the Treaty of Passarowitz; Venice retains only the Ionian Islands and the Dalmatian Coast.

1764 Italian economist Cesare Bo'nesana condemns capital punishment and torture in his influential and widely translated *Tratto de Delittie delle Pene (On Crimes and Punishment).*

1700~1830

Meanwhile, in Venice...

Papa Goldoni, Nasty Snr Gozzi and Alfieri

'Papa' Carlo Goldoni, painted by Alessandro Longhi. 'Here's the table I write on.'

Unfortunately, before the end of the seventeenth century, Italy, like Germany, had come under the baleful influence of French theatrical ideas. But, although its best designers and actors had defected to Paris, all was not lost. A new theatrical form, opera buffa (comic opera – er... aren't they all?) appeared out of the Teatro dei Fioretini in Naples. Opera paid well, which must have been the only reason Venetian Carlo GOLDONI *(1707–93), the first major Italian professional dramatist and brilliant reformer of comedy, wrote opera librettas between plays. After all, why do actors do commercials?*

Goldoni's plays basically brought together the spirit of the commedia dell'arte with the skills of play-writing. He wrote many different types of comedy, exploiting low and high, character and plot. His best works, such as *La Donna Serpente* (*The Snake Woman*), *I Rusteghi* (*The Boors*, 1755), and *Arlecchino, Servitore di Due Padroni* (*The Servant of Two Masters*, 1745), all demonstrate a highly developed sense of theatrical craftsmanship, a sharp social conscience in the satirizing of the upper classes, and clear respect for dialect and local character.

He has been called the Italian Molière partly because he took the French writer as his model, but he never equalled him because he was far too nice to attack miscreant characters with the same joyful vitriol as Molière (he wasn't called Papa Goldoni for nothing: unfortunately niceness and posterity tend not to mix).

A Natural

One of Goldoni's problems in trying to breathe new life into the old commedia material was finding good enough actors. One such was Antonio Sacchi (1708–88) who played Arlecchino. Known as Truffaldino, Sacchi was an actor 'people crowded to see'. He could improvize on the maxims of Cicero and Montaigne, yet 'ally them to the simplicity of the blockhead': a rare talent indeed. Not something learnt at drama school.

1778 La Scala theatre in Milan is built; it will be subsidized by season-ticket holders who will control its policies.

1790 A meteorite shower falls in south-western France; despite samples and 300 statements, the Académie Française declares the shower to be a 'physically impossible phenomenon'.

1827 Italian poet and novelist Alessandro Manzoni finishes *I Promessi Sposi*; the novel, thought to be the greatest Italian prose work since Boccaccio, will not be published until 1840.

Alfieri, by Fabre. 'I see Italians speaking quietly and sitting still. I must be ill.'

The aristocratic *Count Carlo* GOZZI (1720–1806) hated Goldoni because of the latter's tampering with tradition, and his public criticism and carping finally drove Goldoni to Paris in 1762. Amazingly, Gozzi's dreadfully pretentious *Turandot* (1762) went down well throughout Europe, especially Germany (mind you, they would happily have stuck pins in their eyes as an alternative to snobby French Neo-Classicism). He remained connected to the theatre for just four years, after which he withdrew, grumbling and muttering about nasty changes in Italian life.

Vittorio ALFIERI (1749–1803) was the most esteemed serious Italian dramatist. His vision was of a more dignified and intellectually refined drama, classical yet modern in its nationalist flavour. He attempted to replace the excess and flamboyance of Italian acting with restraint and delicacy. He wasn't very successful: he might as well have been asking them to talk without moving their hands, and would have used his time far more effectively if he had relocated to Japan.

Behind the Scenes

As the 18th century began, Venice had about 14 active theatres; by the beginning of the 19th, every city in Italy had at least one. Innovation in architecture, mechanical devices and design in regular theatres (opera houses remained as sumptuous as ever) continued, but the ostentatious 17th-century extravagances began to be replaced by elements of delicacy and refinement. More naturalistic and rustic landscapes decorated the stage (production budgets were a bit thinner, perhaps).

Supporting Roles

One good reason why hardly a decent play came out of 18th-century Italy is that most male playwrights used up all their energy between the bedsheets. **Vincenzo Monti** *(1754–1828),* **Giovanni Pindemonte** *(1751–1812) and* **Nicolo Ugo Foscolo** *(1778–1827) were all more famous for their well-documented love lives than for their scribblings. Well, it's all a question of priorities, isn't it?*

Truffaldino in Gozzi's *The Love for Three Oranges*, ENO, 1989.

1777 Frederick the Great declares, 'It is disgusting to note the increase in the quantity of coffee used by my subjects... My people must drink beer.'

1782 Young German poet Schiller, having left his regiment without permission to attend a performance of his play *Die Räuber*, is arrested and condemned to write only medical treatises.

1791-2 Poland defiantly proclaims a new constitution; by 1795 it will have disappeared from the map, absorbed by its three powerful neighbours, Russia, Prussia and Austria.

1770~1830

Sturm und Drang!

Von Klinger, Goethe and Schiller

In the 1770s, several things happened which had far-reaching long-term effects on German theatre. Christoph Wieland's translations of Shakespeare into German achieved decent productions on the German stage; Rousseau's 'natural' philosophy and Romanticism were given serious consideration; and finally the American Revolution took place, which fired the imagination of anyone in Europe under the age of 30. One consequence of all this was that old Pickleherring was finally given the elbow and German theatre began to think; a period of wild literary excitement ensued and passion made a dramatic entrance.

Goethe on the ice, by Maximilian von Brentano. While he oozes Sturm und Drang machismo, at least one of the ladies is a budding critic.

A group of Young Turks from Strassburg University, including the young Goethe, began an essentially Romantic movement dedicated to Shakespeare and all things 'natural', 'folksy', 'primitive', 'naïve' or in any way anti-Enlightenment, anti-tradition and anti-authority. They found a name for their artistic revolution in the title of a wild fantasy written in Shakespearean prose by *Freidrich Maximillian* VON KLINGER (1752–1831) called *Sturm und Drang* (*Storm and Stress*, 1776). Rebels and figures from mythology became dramatic heroes. Satan, Faust and Prometheus all descended onto the stage to terrify audiences into the realization that humans were fallible, weak, yet potentially heroic – so a good time was guaranteed for all.

The acknowledged master of Sturm und Drang was *Johann Wolfgang* VON GOETHE

1800 Romantic German poet Novalis (Friedrich von Hardenberg), publishes *Hymnen* and *Die Nacht*; he explores the death wish and symbolizes Romantic yearnings as 'the blue flower'.

1814 Eau de cologne becomes fashionable in England; originally called Aqua Mirabilis, the perfumed water has been sold as a sideline by a firm of Italian silk dealers based in Cologne.

1830 German chemist Justus von Liebig and US chemist Samuel Guthrie independently discover the anaesthetic properties of chloric ether, or chloroform.

(1749–1832). He had great ideas but was too untheatrical to write decent plays. His principal work, *Faust*, took from 1775 to 1832 to complete (and was published posthumously).

An early version, *Urfaust*, was influenced by Hans Sachs' theatrical style. Goethe's *Faust* was different to Marlowe's in that whereas the latter wanted unlimited power, Goethe's sought inner understanding of the mystery of life. (That's progress.) He also wrote *Götz von Berlichingen* (1773), the story of a 16th-century Robin Hood-like robber, *Clavigo* (1774), *Stella* (1776), and umpteen novels and poems.

Friedrich SCHILLER (1759–1805) was a close friend of Goethe's and, although Goethe wasn't always so friendly, the two influenced one another all their lives.

Schiller, painted just before he wrote *Don Carlos*; hence the dreamy expression.

Working with animals

Despite his love for them, there was one woman who nearly drove Goethe mad. He was manager of the Weimar Court Theatre when the spoilt and demanding actress Karoline Jagemann arrived. She insisted that he put on *The Dog of Montargis*, a French nonsense which featured a poodle in the lead role. Goethe resigned his job in disgust. He obviously wasn't an animal lover.

PROMPT BOX

The play, *Sturm und Drang*, was originally to be called *Der Wirrwarr* (*The Hurly-Burly*). It was the odd Swiss writer Christoph Kaufmann who suggested the change and he clearly had the gift of foresight. Somehow a revolutionary literary and theatre movement called Wirrwarr! or Hurly-Burly! doesn't have quite the same authority about it.

Supporting Roles

Writers of Sturm und Drang plays either went mad or gave it up for safer activities like life. You think I'm joking? **Jakob Lenz** *(1751–92) idolized Goethe to such an extent he became a social embarrassment. Obviously very confused, he died in an asylum.* **Friedrich von Klinger** *left theatre after a few years and ended up a general in the Russian army.*

Schiller's plays, *Die Räuber* (*The Robbers*, 1781), *Fiesco* (1783) and *Kabale und Liebe* (*Intrigue and Love*, 1784), were all Sturm und Drang plays full of passion, patriots and avengers of the oppressed. Later he wrote *Don Carlos*, 1787, a much quieter romantic drama of social change, followed by the *Wallenstein* trilogy (1799), giving Germany one of its most outstanding and durable stage characters. Coleridge liked Wallenstein so much, he translated it into English.

1699–1712 Castle Howard, an imposing baroque mansion, is built in Yorkshire; its architect is English playwright Sir John Vanbrugh.

1745 The British Excise Act taxes glass by weight; less lead is used in glass manufacture, drinking glasses become smaller and more highly decorated, especially on the stem.

1760 The Archbishop of Canterbury forces the Drury Lane Theatre management to remove the line, 'You snub-nose son of a bitch' from the play *The Minor*.

1696~1815

Handsome Rogues

Cibber, Garrick, Sheridan, *et al.*

Colley Cibber: 'Hello, my darlings! Would anyone like this nose hair as a memento?'

One eighteenth-century theatre development was the amount of hot air in print by and about actors and managers. Reminiscences, criticism and diaries proliferated from every thespian (and, methinks, every orifice). Colley CIBBER *(1671–1757) penned* An Apology For The Life of Colley Cibber, Comedian *in 1740 ('Apology' here means 'account', though either meaning would do). This provided one of the most complete accounts ever written of the lot of the luvvie. Cibber began as a comic actor under Thomas Betterton at Drury Lane, wrote some mediocre plays and became actor-manager at Drury Lane and the Haymarket. George II made him poet laureate. It pays to be a windbag (a useful tip to remember, I find).*

Flouting the Law

The Licensing Act of 1737, continuing the monopoly created by the Royal Patents in London, limited legal playhouses to Covent Garden, Drury Lane and the Haymarket. It was engineered by the loathsome Sir Robert Walpole to censor writers like Henry Fielding who, in his burlesque comedies, reminded the public of Walpole's corruption. The Act made all other theatres illegal, a status they blithely ignored. Bribes helped keep the local economies going.

In terms of acting, *David* GARRICK (1717–79) was simply the best, and he got everyone to agree with him. Samuel Johnson, James Boswell and the painter Joshua Reynolds all adored Garrick in their memoirs. Garrick could act any character, was a dramatist, adapted Shakespeare, and dazzled London society with his brilliance, wit and talent. There had never been anyone like him in English theatre. As manager of Drury Lane (1747–76) he elevated theatre to new heights of professional discipline (i.e. actors arrived on time and sober). If he'd had time, he'd probably have solved the

1764 In protest at contemporary vulgarity, a group of young Englishmen form the Macaroni Club, where extreme sensibility and effeminacy in dress prevail.

1773 The Royal Society gives Joseph Priestley a medal; through experimenting with the carbon dioxide produced by a neighbouring brewery, he has invented soda water.

1813 A Russian navy captain visiting Japanese shops sees prepackaged and prepriced goods – something as yet unknown in the West.

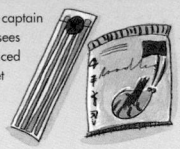

PROMPT BOX

The first Covent Garden Theatre opened in 1732, thus sharing monopoly with Drury Lane, which itself enlarged in 1787 to 2,000 capacity, and to 3,600 at the end of the century. English theatres had no 'stacks' of Italian boxes. Instead, balconies were spread wide and deep and walls fanned out from the stage to increase capacity and revenue. Thus did greed create bad sightlines and bellowing actors – and still does.

Mystery of Life (as it was, he just pioneered modern theatre management).

Another handsome rogue was *Richard Brinsley* SHERIDAN (1751–1816), who wrote several brilliant comedies, including *The Rivals*, 1775, *School for Scandal*, 1777 and *The Critic; or A Tragedy Rehearsed*, 1779; but he was more interested in political fame. Most of his resources were channelled into getting him into Parliament (the best show in town, after all). He bought the Drury Lane theatre in 1776 but didn't look after it, so it fell into disrepair and had to be rebuilt in 1791. It reopened in 1794 and, with the help of actors Mrs Siddons and John Philip Kemble, became a success.

It burned down in 1809, and Sheridan had to rebuild again. This time, as it burned, Sheridan sat in a café across the street. When friends asked him what he was doing, he remonstrated, 'Can a man not warm himself by his own fire?'

Actor *John Philip* KEMBLE (1757–1823) managed Drury Lane under Sheridan, and went on to Covent Garden where his sister, *Sarah* SIDDONS (1755–1831), gave many a memorable performance. In 1808 Covent Garden burned down (careless then, weren't they!), and after rebuilding it Kemble and Siddons tried to recoup losses by raising admission prices. This provoked the 'Old Price Riots' which devastated performances for three months.

Supporting Roles

John Gay (1685–1732) wrote The Beggar's Opera *in 1728 (which inspired Bertholt Brecht to create* The Threepenny Opera *with music by Kurt Weill). Another theatrical Irishman was Robert Wilks, who was so loved in Ireland that the Lord Lieutenant issued a warrant to prevent his leaving the country. Oliver Goldsmith's* She Stoops to Conquer, *1773, is frequently revived today.*

Captain Macheath, the gallant highwayman two women fight over in *The Beggar's Opera*.

1751 The young George Washington visits Barbados and samples its tropical fruit; 'none pleases my taste as do's the pine [pineapple]'.

1764 Houses are numbered for the first time in London.

1769 Spanish Franciscan Father Junipero Serra plants the first wine grapes, oranges, figs and olives in California at the newly founded Mission of San Diego de Alcala.

1750~1815

The Brits on Tour II: America

Kean & Murray, Hallam, Fennell and Cooper

Due largely to the religious ideals of the Puritans and the Quakers, American theatre was rather slow in getting off the ground. So virtually all actors of note were English, French or Italian tourists. This was a time when Puritan critics with funny names made the rules; people like 'Increase Mather' (no sane person calls their son 'Increase'; he in turn called his son Cotton), who complained of the 'gynecandrical dancing' on stage.

Not just an elaborate hunch: Thomas Kean's Richard III was said to carry the Drury Lane Theatre.

In 1750, the Commonwealth of Massachusetts passed a law banning theatrical performances and their 'painted vanities', whilst New England zealots billed *Othello* as 'A Series of Moral Dialogues, in Five Parts, Depicting the Evils of Jealousy and Other Bad Passions'. I blame it on chafing underwear.

Not all America was so hostile. Virginia, Charleston and Philadelphia, for example, had their own small theatres and provided a base for visiting English companies. Thomas Kean and William Murray toured a company to Philadelphia in 1749, and opened *Richard III* in New York in 1750 with Kean as Richard. The first well-organized company to visit America was made up of 12 English actors (who couldn't get jobs in England!), brought together by William Hallam. They opened at Williamsburg in 1752 with *The Merchant of Venice*. A year later they moved to New York. But as yet no real 'stars' had visited America, and didn't until the attitude began to perceptibly change towards the end of the century.

Kean 'blacked up' to play Othello – and looked pretty ridiculous.

1773 In protest against the British tax on tea, Bostonians board three British ships and empty their cargo of tea into Boston Harbor.

1783 American lexicographer Noah Webster publishes his *American Spelling Book*, which will help to standardize American spelling. His *Dictionary* will be published in 1828.

1803 Maryland farmer Thomas Moore patents the first icebox; it will be in common use by 1838.

The first 'big name' to visit was an ex-Covent Garden tragedian, *James* FENNELL (1766–1816), who became an instant success on his arrival in Philadelphia in 1792, playing roles like Othello and Lear. He made a lot of money but invested it unwisely and, after a spell in prison for debt, died poor and mad (perhaps he was the first real Method actor). *Thomas Abthorpe* COOPER (1776–1849), although not so successful in London as Fennell had been, was considered excellent in his 1796 American debut as Macbeth at the Chestnut Street Theatre in Philadelphia. He discarded the American stock system in favour of travelling from one company to another performing only star roles. In 1801 he moved to the Park Street theatre in New York and five years later joined its management.

Supporting Roles

George Frederick Cooke *(1756–1811), star of Covent Garden in 1800–3, specialized in meaty satanic roles like Richard III, Shylock, Iago and Sir Giles Overreach. Widely considered to be Kemble's only serious rival, he might have gone on to even greater things had it not been for the demon alcohol. Cooper persuaded him to try his luck in America, and, when sober, he was apparently brilliant – when drunk a liability, albeit an entertaining one.*

What's in a Name?

Not surprisingly, when the Revolution became imminent, there was increasing antagonism towards English actors. Even the fact that David Douglass, after taking over from William Hallam, changed the name of the Company of London Comedians to the American Company of Comedians didn't impress the locals. By the 1770s, many states banned theatre altogether and most English actors wisely scurried off for Jamaica.

Cooper as Richmond (to Kean as Richard III): 'Go on, admit it! My sideburns are better.'

1821 English actor Junius Brutus Booth goes to the United States to play Richard III in Richmond, Virginia, and settles; one of his two actor sons will assassinate Abraham Lincoln.

1827 Parisian students introduce the Mardi Gras (Shrove Tuesday) celebration to New Orleans.

1832 The stage musical *Jim Crow* wins 20 encores at the City Theatre in Louisville, Kentucky.

1815~1905

The First Age of the American Actors

Payne, Forrest, the Booths and those Barrymores

When it did get going, American theatre raced ahead. Plenty of good actors and actresses appeared and theatre buildings increased from a mere handful in 1800 to five thousand by 1885. Good writers came later – evidence that the most fundamental element of any theatre is the live presence of the actor (the live presence of an audience has also been known to help).

PROMPT BOX

The American Minstrelsy Show, where white men mocked Negroes by blacking their faces and singing stupid songs, was popularized by Thomas D. Rice (1806–60). He introduced the 'comic' Negro character Jim Crow to the stage. Despite its crass racism, 'minstrelsy' continued up to the 1960s, with the televised 'Black and White Minstrel Show'.

Rice as Jim Crow (Bowery, New York, 1833). Note 'enlightened' all-white audience, crowds on stage (some fighting) and tacky backdrop.

John Payne (1791–1852) was the first American star. He also published the first American theatre journal, *The Thespian Mirror*, in 1804, before he was 15 years old. (However, he had his off days, such as when he wrote the kitsch popular song 'Home, Sweet Home').

Edwin Forrest (1806–1872) was the first American-born actor to achieve fame abroad. This 'vast animal bewildered by a grain of genius' appeared at many of the finest American theatres before attempting to beat the English in their own backyard in 1836. The response was sneering contempt (the English treat foreigners, new ideas and rabies alike), and the worst came from fellow thespians. Shaken but not deterred, he returned to America and went on to greater things.

1861–5 The American Civil War will take more than 600,000 lives, destroy property worth $5 billion, buy freedom for four million slaves and leave a legacy of bitterness in the South.

1868 Alcatraz, the island off San Francisco, is first used as a prison. No one ever escapes and lives to tell the tale.

1900 Mark Twain returns to the United States after ten years' absence; the *New York Times* hails him as 'the Hero as Man of Letters'.

Booth as Hamlet (1864) looking for his brother in the stalls. He gave 100 consecutive performances.

Edwin BOOTH (1855–93) has been called the best actor of 19th-century America. If this is true, then his brother, John Wilkes, had to be the worst spectator. Edwin came from an interesting family and led a life crowded with incident: daddy went mad, so did brother and wife, other brother killed President, nephew killed someone else, Winter Garden (which he managed) burned down, and finally he went bankrupt. After John Wilkes Booth shot Lincoln, the family got no more invitations to barbecues, so Edwin had to retire.

In 1866 he ventured nervously back onstage, worried there might be someone like his brother out there. But before he had spoken a word, the audience burst into applause (they had either decided he was blameless or reappraised Lincoln).

The Barrymore dynasty began with a Mrs *DREW* (1820–97), who made pots of money managing the Arch Street theatre in Philadelphia. Her son John was a comedian and her daughter, Georgie, married Maurice Barrymore (real name Herbert Blythe). Their marriage produced Lionel, John and Ethel, later called the 'royal family of Broadway', all of whom started in stage classics and moved to film.

Supporting Roles

James Hackett *(1800–71) played Falstaff to great acclaim in New York and in England.* **Robert Montgomery Bird** *(1806–54) won a thousand-dollar prize (offered by Edwin Forrest to stimulate American writing) with* The Gladiator *(1831).* **Ira Aldridge** *(1810–66) was one of the first American black actors. He was [illegible] to Edmund Kean and eventually played Othello in Russia and England.*

1802 Mme Tussaud's museum of waxworks opens in London; the Swiss wax modeller made death masks of famous guillotine victims in Paris during the Reign of Terror.

1802 In London, only Covent Garden and Drury Lane theatres are licensed for the performance of drama; too large to permit subtlety and naturalism, they rely on spectacle and melodrama.

1826 Louis Jacques Mandé Daguerre, who has been painting scenery for the Paris Opéra, approaches J.N. Niepce and proposes a partnership.

1800~1870

Horrid Little Men

Kean, Kemble, Vestris

Edmund KEAN (1787–1833), later called genius, brilliant etc., had a rather uninspiring start. His parentage is unknown but he was said to have had an 'adventurous childhood'. In 1807, aged 20, he was described by his overbearing co-star, Mrs Siddons, as a 'horrid little man' of whom there was 'too little... to make a great actor'. Was she ever wrong!

Edmund Kean playing Richard III at the Garrick Club, looking more like Ali Baba than the King of England.

Kean revolutionized acting by sudden transitions from 'low' to 'high' in his delivery, which is what Coleridge alluded to when he said watching Kean was like 'reading Shakespeare by flashes of lightning'. Later in his life these 'flashes' dimmed as he succumbed to fame, booze and sex. He burned himself out aged 44 (but what a life!). His son, Charles, was also an actor but one with the charisma and talent of a fence post.

Charles KEMBLE (1775–1854), younger brother of John Philip (also a thesp), was a handsome actor who managed Covent Garden. But he spent too much money and his daughter, *Fanny KEMBLE* (1809–93), had to act (which she hated) to bail him out. *Lucia VESTRIS* (1797–1856) was a 'breeches' actress, which means she played men's roles – a tradition extending in England to the 'principal boy' in modern pantomime. She later managed the Olympic Theatre.

Behind the Scenes

Lucia Vestris promoted the box set, probably a French import, with its realistic 'room-like' setting containing real doors, furniture and a ceiling instead of hanging 'borders'. She used these sets in her productions of *A Midsummer Night's Dream*, *London Assurance* by Boucicault, and Gay's *The Beggar's Opera*. Multiple sets also appeared where several 'rooms' were visible at the same time, a device used by the likes of Alan Ayckbourn in the 20th century (see page 121).

Seeking the Limelight

'Limelight' was a form of lighting from 1816. A piece of limestone was heated with a mixture of gases and, if reflected by a mirror, became an intense spotlight. After 1860 the auditorium could be darkened and just the stage lit by using piped gas, which could be extinguished and relit with electric sparks.

1830 Irish inventor Aeneas Coffee patents the continuous still, which speeds up the distilling process for whiskey and gin and produces a purer spirit.

1847-8 Under the pseudonyms Currer, Ellis and Acton Bell, the three Brontë sisters, Charlotte, Emily and Anne, publish their first novels *Jane Eyre*, *Wuthering Heights* and *Agnes Grey*.

51848 Retired schoolteacher Dorothea Lynde Dix informs the US Congress of over 9,000 epileptics and insane persons who are being maltreated in insane asylums.

Before the monopoly of the patent theatres was abolished in 1843, 'minor' theatres were permitted to put on pantomimic and musical shows. These had to comprise three acts only (five were for the 'legitimate' playhouses) and could contain five or six songs but absolutely no spoken dialogue (from this we get the 'musical'). However, dialogue crept in (in 1832 *Othello* was performed, with an occasional plonk from a piano to make it legal) and, to compete with the successful 'minor' theatres, Drury Lane and Covent Garden put on ever more spectacular shows. Ships exploded and sank, buildings burned, fire engines raced across the stage. Covent Garden once filled the entire stage area with water for *The Cataract of the Ganges*, and a cannon explosion at Drury Lane killed a member of the audience (hence the famous Drury Lane ghost).

Supporting Roles

This was also the time of the great clown **Joseph Grimaldi** *(1779–1837), the 'King of Clowns'. Famous for his white make-up with two red half-moons on the cheeks, he was best known as Harlequin in* Mother Goose *also performed as* The Golden Egg *(Covent Garden, 1806). His antics and talent became the benchmark for all clowns since, many of whom visit his Pentonville grave annually to this day.*

In 1817, gaslight arrived on the stage. Conveyed by miles of rubber tubing, it could take controlled light to anywhere in the theatre. However, the fumes accumulated beneath the roof and those sitting in the 'gods' sometimes fainted or even expired (theatre-goers were so much more *dedicated* in those days). It also caused many fires; nearly 400 theatres burned down in America and Europe during the century.

Grimaldi in *The Red Dwarf*. After killing Pantaloon, he dresses him as Lion, Ass, Eagle, Cat and Fish.

1852-4 Isambard Kingdom Brunel and Sir Matthew Wyatt design Paddington Station in London; the structure combines glass and iron and has additional decorative details.

1857 The Indian Mutiny begins when both Hindu and Muslim soldiers in the British Army refuse to bite open greased rifle cartridges, believing them to be coated with taboo animal fat.

1860 Boucicault's play *The Colleen Bawn, or the Brides of Garryowen*, premieres.

1850~1900

The Actor and the Manager

Macready, Phelps, Bancroft, Irving, Terry

The nineteenth century saw a growth in Europe and America of the actor-manager of larger and more financially viable theatres. Yet hardly any decent plays were written. Experimentation, when it came later in the century, veered towards Naturalism and Realism, which were sweeping over Europe and America.

The hot-tempered *William MACREADY* (1793–1873) was an actor who managed Covent Garden before Lucia Vestris. He encouraged the poet Robert Browning and novelist Edward Bulwer-Lytton to write for the stage (but he really shouldn't have bothered). *Samuel PHELPS* (1804–78) took on Sadler's Wells, a home of melodrama that had fallen into disrepair. He staged only melodramas by the best – Dion Boucicault and Tom Taylor, plus Elizabethan and Jacobean plays – and his approach turned the fortunes of Sadler's around. Lilian Baylis later used his example as a model for her revival of the Old Vic.

PROMPT BOX

Ellen Terry allowed Irving to dominate her career, something which so incensed George Bernard Shaw he began a long and loving correspondence with her. Unhappily married, her illicit affair with the married architect E.W. Godwin produced two children, one of whom was Edward Gordon Craig (see page 104), and one of her great nephews is Sir John Gielgud. So Irving did something useful.

Irving as Henry VIII. His elocution and gait were supposedly rather 'mannered'.

In the spotlight

Irving was such an egotist he wanted to establish the Lyceum as a centre of acting excellence – with himself as the most excellent. It is rumoured that any lighting technician who did not focus the spotlight exclusively on Irving, even when he was standing to one side whilst another actor was speaking, was dismissed. I'm sure it's just a rumour. But in any case, what's the point of being the star if people can't see you shine?

1883 English juries convict 12,000 people, while magistrates send 80,000 to jail without trial.

1890 English soap manufacturer William Lever builds a Sunlight soap factory and creates the model industrial town of Port Sunlight.

1900 English actress Mrs Patrick Campbell appears in Frank Harris' *Mr and Mrs Daventry*, based on an idea purchased from Oscar Wilde who dies in the same year.

Sir Squire BANCROFT (1841–1926), whose name sounds like a character in a Jacobean farce, his wife, Marie Wilton, and the playwright *Tom* ROBERTSON (1829–71), are all credited with the first development of Naturalism/Realism on the English stage.

W.S. Gilbert, a lawyer by training. 'I am a doggerel bard' runs the refrain to one of his ballads.

Robertson's plays, *Ours* (1866), *Caste* (1867) and *School* (1869), produced by the Bancrofts at the Prince of Wales Theatre, were all styled realistically in setting and language. Detractors dubbed them 'cup and saucer' dramas (since Robertson had put real tea on stage; but by the way, stage whisky is... yes, you've got it... real tea).

The big guns of the century were *Sir Henry* IRVING (1838–1905), the first actor to be knighted, and *Dame Ellen* TERRY (1874–1928). Irving ran the Lyceum from 1878 until his production of *Macbeth* in 1888, which failed and almost ruined him (not unlike Peter O'Toole in 1980 – powerful stuff, that Scottish play). He was an egotistical actor whose only criterion in selecting the plays he wanted to show was whether they had terrific parts for him to play. On the other hand, Ellen Terry, whom Irving kept firmly in his shadow, was a genuinely marvellous actress.

The 'well-made play' came largely from the pens of French writers *Eugène* SCRIBE (1791–1861) and *Victorien* SARDOU (1831–1908). Scribe wrote more than 350 plays. Originating in the comedy of intrigue, they were crafted to arouse suspense by starting with a detailed exposition of plot and then developing crises and complications before a climactic ending. It is a basic formula that has influenced theatre in the West ever since.

The D'Oyly Carte Company

'With some music and librettas, they produced their operettas. Even if they're mediocre, they earned lots of filthy lucre.' See, it's easy! William Gilbert and Arthur Sullivan together with Rupert D'Oyly Carte formed the D'Oyly Carte Company and created a series of silly operettas. After the success of *Trial by Jury* (1875) and *HMS Pinafore* (1878) they produced 12 other crowd-pullers at the Savoy.

Arthur Sullivan. As well as operettas, he wrote the tune for the hymn 'Onward Christian Soldiers'.

Supporting Roles

It is said the Irish-American **Dion Boucicault** *invented the touring system per se. Arriving in America in 1853, he fought to protect the legal rights of authors. He achieved some basic 'sole rights' for authors, reducing the theft of plays by actors/managers, and sent several companies on tour to act his plays without star performers, hence the 'touring' system.*

1835 Karl Schinkel, inspired by the medieval castles he has seen in England, builds the picturesque Schloss Babelsberg in Germany.

1851 Franz Dingelstedt becomes Director of the Munich Theatre; his elaborate productions will make theatrical history.

1862 Otto von Bismarck becomes Prussian premier; under his rule, Prussia will defeat Austria and take leadership over the newly created North German Confederation.

1830~1900

Nationalism vs Naturalism

Büchner, Saxe-Meinengen, Wagner

Ibsen's *Ghosts* shocked contemporary audiences and set new standards in acting.

Bored by the escapist ramblings of the Romantics, another group of young German lads tried to create a more dynamic, nationalistic theatre, to take up where Sturm und Drang left off. They formed the Junges Deutschland (Young Germany) movement of the 1830s and 1840s. Unfortunately censorship and the dominance of the well-made play dampened their ardour.

Of their writers, *Georg BÜCHNER* (1813–37) was considered one of the best. A revolutionary, he died of typhoid at 24. *Danton's Death* (1835), though brilliant, was never played in his lifetime. Neither was the portion of a work entitled *Woyzeck*, (1836) which Alban Berg turned into an opera after World War I.

PROMPT BOX

The Freie Buehne was modelled on the French Théâtre-libre (see page 79) which also influenced Stanislavsky's Moscow Arts Theatre. It was followed by the Freie Volksbuehne (Free People's Stage) established by Bruno Wille in 1890. Wille went on to found the Neue Freie Buehne (New Free Stage) in 1892 which survived until 1933 despite many police and State attempts to close it.

GEORGE II, Duke of Saxe-Meinengen (1826–1914), unintentionally brought about one of the biggest changes in Western theatre when he challenged the

1876 The Reichsbank is opened; it will play an important role in German economic development.

1895 Bavarian physicist Wilhelm Roentgen discovers X-rays; it will now be possible to photograph the internal organs of animals and humans.

1897-1900 Ferdinan Count von Zeppelin invents the first airship or rigid type dirigible balloon; the Zeppelin will be used by Germany in the First World War.

dire German practice of 'big' solo acting with crowd scenes played like wooden opera choruses. He introduced ensemble acting, 'the collective personality of the group', which by default brought the stage director (or Chief Luvvy) to the fore. The Meinengen Players visited nine countries between 1874 and 1890 and were seen by all the major figures in theatre, some of whom, like Stanislavsky, were to develop these ideas further.

A self-styled 'total man of the theatre' and revolutionary, *Richard WAGNER* (1813–83) argued that theatre should be Gesamtkunstwerk, or 'total artwork'.

Supporting Roles

Heinrich Laube *(1806–84) and* **Karl Gutzkow** *(1811–79) were the leaders of the Young Germany movement. Gutzkow wrote* Uriel Acosta *(1847), the seminal work of the group, reflecting its liberal sentiments. When he was imprisoned for 'political offences', Laube, who had also spent nine months in jail for openly supporting the French Revolution, turned against the movement. He later changed his allegiance and leaned to the right politically.*

Richard Wagner: his ideas, like his personality, were on a grand scale.

Whilst this theory was undoubtedly brilliant and influenced the future direction of theatre design, in practice it was only partly successful since his staging tended always to be typical of 'spectacle theatre'. His most famous work was the *Ring of the Nibelings* cycle (1853–74). Wagner's opus has caused controversy since the first performances and he has often been accused of violent anti-Semitism and vigorous pro-Nazism. Naturalism finally gained a hold in Germany with the so-called Freie Buehne, or 'free stage' of Otto Brahm. Created as a subscription organization to avoid censorship by the police, who wouldn't allow the bourgeois to be offended (some things never change), it opened for business with Ibsen's *Ghosts* in 1889 and lasted for only three seasons. But it had set the German Naturalism revolution in motion, inspiring many imitators in its wake.

1830 Parisian M. Croisat revives the hairdressing profession by introducing the '1830 Mode', an elaborate style requiring professional skill.

1840 French socialist Pierre Joseph Proudhon, in his treatise *Qu'est-ce que la propriété?*, declares that, 'Property is theft'.

1851 The majority of French people have endorsed by plebiscite the new constitution introduced by Louis Napoleon after his coup.

1830~1900

Romanticism vs Naturalism

Hugo, De Musset, Sardou, Bernhardt and Antoine

Victor Hugo photographed in 1875.

It hardly seems possible to us now that the style of a stage play should cause a riot. But Hernani *by Victor Hugo (1802–85) did. It opened at the Comédie Française in 1830 and upset the delicate French aesthetes in three ways: it scorned the classical unities, it contained popular theatre devices, and, third, it was written by a man who was already despised as the leading Romantic and an anti-establishment political writer (something for everyone). He had previously set out the theoretical basis for Romantic drama in the preface to his play* Cromwell *(1827), claiming elements of the sublime and grotesque could be combined in the same play (Oh! The rascal!). Alfred* DE MUSSET *(1810–57), a better dramatist than Hugo, wrote mainly to be read. But they reached the stage anyway and have been revived many times since.*

PROMPT BOX

The great French actress Rachel was actually Swiss and her real name was Elisa Felix. As a child she was so poor she sang on the streets until she was 11, when the musician Alexandre Étienne Choron took her under his protection. She then went to the *Conservatoire* and thence to the Comédie.

The subject matter of the 'well-made plays' of Eugene Scribe and Victorien Sardou (see page 75) was the bourgeoisie, while situation and 'intrigue' tended to dominate character development. Bernard Shaw disliked them intensely, coining the rude epithet 'Sardoodledum' – but he could be an old misery, and made a career out of being cantankerous.

Nevertheless, the actress *Sarah* BERNHARDT (1844–1923) achieved her reputation in Sardou's plays at the Comédie Française, especially *Théodora* (1884). She also took the title role of de Musset's Shakespearean drama *Lorenzaccio* (written 1834) in 1896. From 1880 Bernhardt toured England, Denmark, Russia, North and South

1858 The Bibliothèque Nationale (national library) opens to the public in Paris.

1869 The butter substitute margarine is developed by French chemist Hippolyte Mège-Mouri's. British dairy farmers try to get a bill passed requiring it to be coloured purple.

1900 Economic necessity forces French artist Henri Matisse to paint decorations for the Paris Exposition.

Supporting Roles

For the Romantics, **Edmond Rostand** *(with* Cyrano de Bergerac, *1897 – 50 years after the Romantic movement had died), and* **Alexandre Dumas *père*** (Henry III and his court, *1827). For the Realists/Naturalists,* **Alexandre Dumas *fils*** (Le Demi-monde, *1855),* **Emile Zola** (Thérèse Raquin, *1867),* **Henry Becque** (The Vultures, *1882) and the most 'naturalistic' of all,* **Eugène Brieux** (The Red Robe, *1900).*

America and Australia, then drove everyone mad with endless 'farewell' performances – the last few of which she performed after having her leg amputated.

The person who probably did most to advance Naturalism/Realism on the stage was a young Paris gas company clerk and amateur actor called *André* ANTOINE (1858–1943). In 1887 he rented a hall and began a 'free' theatre – the *Théâtre-libre*, a private playhouse open only to subscribers. For eight years he produced experimental playwrights who weren't granted productions elsewhere. He went further than Saxe-Meinengen, too, in making his actors speak and move as real people, sometimes having them speak lines with their backs to the audience. He used realistic settings with real food and everyday furniture. (Now theatre can be as dull as being at home!)

Crowd Trouble

For the opening night of *Hernani* Hugo (1802–85) dispensed with his paid claque of supporters, counting on the 'artists of Paris', who loved him, to help. They turned out in velvet suits and floppy hats to combat the 'classicists' who hissed and sang at the top of their voices. Then they all set to blows. These days they might prefer a football match, although they would be advised to change their strip.

Going Bust

Although Antoine's Théâtre-libre had, by 1890, presented to the French the first performances of plays by Ibsen, Tolstoy, Strindberg and Hauptmann and had over 12,000 articles written about it, it was in financial ruin. In 1894, unable to make a profit and owing some 100,000 francs, he turned it over to another director.

Sarah Bernhardt as Cleopatra: 'This is my best side.'

1820 Italian author Alessandro Manzoni's historical verse tragedy *Carmagnola* completely disregards the Classical 'Unities'; he is the founder of Italian romantic drama.

1839 Naples and Portici are linked by the first Italian railway, which covers a distance of eight kilometres.

1861 Lombardy, Piedmont, Modena, Lucca, Romagna, Tuscany and the two Sicilies unite under Victor Emmanuel II of Piedmont to form the Kingdom of Italy; Venetia and Rome will join later.

1820~1900

Nationalism vs Everyone in Italy

D'Annunzio, Ristori, Duse, Salvini

Italy had one major issue on its mind during the 19th century: becoming Italian. The struggle for unity and independence from the Bourbons, the Papal States and the dreaded French Classicism preoccupied the aristocracy (working people, as always, weren't asked and anyway hadn't time to give a hoot about such things). So Italy's theatre went uncharacteristically quiet.

D'Annunzio fled to France in 1912 to escape a string of creditors who were anxious to talk to him.

When Romanticism arrived it was given a strong nationalistic flavour. Realism had to wait until Italy become a nation in 1870. The Italian version was called Verismo, but differed from French or German Realism in that the Church was very powerful and, Italian men being what they are anyway, there was no talk of women's rights, labour legislation, divorce or liberalizing marriage laws. Heavens no, Italian Realism stuck to really important issues like preserving the lifestyles of the rich! Later Naturalism appeared only in the north, while the south remained stubbornly feudalistic.

PROMPT BOX

D'Annunzio wasn't very generous to Eleonora Duse. Despite her pouring love, talent and money into his projects, he gave the lead role in his first play, *La Città Morta* to Sarah Bernhardt. He later treated Duse so badly before leaving her that both critics and public turned against him. You can't expect to get away with that kind of thing in Italy.

Poet and novelist *Gabriele D'Annunzio* (1863–1938) developed interest in the theatre after developing interest in Eleonora Duse in 1896 (they remained in partnership for some years). D'Annunzio took as his models the Greeks, music drama, Wagner and Nietzsche, but his ambitions for a 'total art form' were never

1865–77 Giuseppe Mengoni designs the Galleria Vittorio Emanuele in Milan; the shopping arcade, in the form of a cross, is the largest and most elegant of its kind in Europe.

1896 The Lumière brothers' film on the city of Venice includes a sequence shot from a moving gondola, similar to the effect of the theatrical roller-panorama.

1900s Spanish-born theatrical innovator and textile artist Mariano Fortuny creates the effect of a natural sky by playing reflected and diffused coloured lights across his revolutionary 'cupola' above the stage.

Supporting Roles

Of the few writers of merit, **Giovanni Niccolini** *(1782–1861) whose propagandist* Nabucco *(1819) targeted Napoleon and religious despotism,* **Alessandro Manzoni** *(1785–1873), whose* Il Conte di Carmagnola *(1820), was influenced by Schiller's* Wallenstein *and* **Paolo Ferrari** *(1822–1873), a comic romantic writer whose* Amore senza Stima *(1868) showed Goldoni's influence, stood out.*

fully realized. *La Città Morta* (1898), *La Gioconda* (1898), and *Francesca da Rimini* (1902) all starred Duse.

Adelaide RISTORI (1821–1906) was a major actress in Europe and America, playing Lady Macbeth opposite Edward Booth. Her major rival was the French actress, Rachel (stage name of *Elisa* FELIX, 1820–58). *Eleonora* DUSE (1858–1924) was the biggest star. She came from a family of actors (born on a train whilst on tour, dontcha know), and made her debut at the age of four in *Les Misérables*. She dominated the European stage, rivalling Bernhardt in America, though her spurning of corsets, hair dye and make-up confused New York socialites. Ristori once called her 'the modern woman, with all her maladies of hysteria, anaemia and neurosis'.

Tommaso SALVINI (1829–1916) was a truly great performer. Also born into a theatrical family, in 1843 he joined a company run by Gustavo Modena, whose tenets of simplicity, naturalness and psychological truth influenced him. Although Salvini acted all the major roles, his Othello was considered the most memorable, especially to his Desdemonas, who apparently found his passion in the smothering scene a bit too realistic.

Tommaso Salvini as a notoriously enthusiastic Othello.

In Character

In part, Konstantin Stanislavsky's decision to formalize actor training was influenced by watching Tommaso Salvini night after night when he was touring Russia. Stanislavsky observed that Salvini uniquely spent an hour or so before going on stage in preparing himself psychologically. This was revolutionary for its time, since actors normally turned up at the theatre just before their character had to be on stage. It's interesting to speculate how he prepared for his well-known Othello. Must have been terrifying for whoever was doing his make-up.

1857 Björnstjerne Björnson precedes Ibsen as a writer of realistic plays dealing with social problems.

1895 Bernard Shaw on *Little Eyolf*: 'how nicely Mrs [Patrick] Campbell took the drowning of the child! Just a pretty waving of the fingers, a moderate scream as if she had very nearly walked on a tin tack!'

1901 The first Nobel prizes are awarded by Alfred Nobel, a successful industrialist who had failed as a novelist and playwright.

1850~1910

Scandinavian Mysticism

Ibsen and the split personality of Strindberg

Strindberg hallucinating.

It is said that Henrik IBSEN *(1828–1906) was a bad-tempered man with few social graces. But what of that? Far better his energies were gainfully employed by an indignant social conscience linked to an enormous talent as a dramatist, than in merely being nice to people.*

In 1866 he wrote a dramatic poem, called *Brand*, a searing attack on meanness, pettiness and compromise. The same anger propelled the writing of the slightly mystic *Peer Gynt* the following year. After this his life and his work became devoted to dramatic realism and left-wing politics, inspired by the social militancy of the Danish critic, Georg Brandes. Ibsen's major works, from *A Doll's House* (1879) to *When We Dead Awaken* (1899), placed him as one of Europe's foremost realistic and socially challenging writers and changed the course of world theatre. *A Doll's House* promoted female emancipation, *Ghosts* (1881) tackled hereditary syphilis and euthanasia, while *Hedda Gabler* (1890) focused on the individual disaster of women who are not yet ready for emancipation.

If ever a man needed a cold plunge pool, it was *August* STRINDBERG (1849–1912). More versatile than Ibsen, he was much troubled spiritually throughout his life, and his genius was clearly tinged with madness (it's a fine line, dear, a fine line...). After teaching, journalism and library work, his writing entered into a Naturalist phase in the 1880s, when he followed Zola, and then a Symbolist/Expressionist phase. In the first he wrote

Peer Gynt (1994, Royal Shakespeare Co.). Sitting astride a pig and definitely off with the trolls.

1905 After 91 years of union, Norway becomes independent of Sweden.

1907 Norway grants its women the right to vote – Britain and the United States will not follow suit until, respectively, 1918 and 1919.

1908 Painter Edvard Munch, after suffering a mental breakdown, settles permanently in Norway; his best-known painting, The Scream (1893), is thought to reflect his childhood trauma.

The Father (1887) and *Miss Julie* (1888); the latter's preface is regarded by some as the manifesto for Naturalism. Actually, it's more about Realism – but more of that later! This early work has been accused of violent misogyny, but that is possibly more revealing of those who like to use fashionable psychological labelling than an insight into a highly subjective writer. From 1889 he ran his own experimental theatre in Copenhagen, modelled on Antoine's Théâtre-libre. However, the following decade he dropped theatre to wrestle with his demons in scientific experiments and occult research. His 'Inferno Crisis', a period of five psychotic episodes, put him in a mental hospital and only reading the philosopher Emmanuel Swedenborg saved his mind. The plays that followed, including the 'To Damascus' trilogy, *The Dance of Death* (1900) and *A Dream Play* (1902), are his best and show incredible diversity and experimentation.

PROMPT BOX

Strindberg, who had 'searched for God and found the Devil', was praised by John Synge, the Irish dramatist, who said 'Strindberg shakes flame from the living planets and the fixed stars. Ibsen can sit serenely in his Doll's House while Strindberg is battling with heaven and hell.' Ibsen himself had remarked about him, 'There is one who will be greater than I.' Such befitting sanguinity.

Supporting Roles

Denmark had **Adam Oehlenschläger** *(1779–1850), who was a great influence on Ibsen, as was* **Johan Heiberg** *(1791–1860). Then there was* **Hans Christian Andersen** *(1805–75) who considered his plays more important than his fairy tales (the world thought otherwise) and* **Hjalmar Bergstrom** *(1868–1914). As a small country, actors often directed, and vice versa, which was nice for them.*

Henrik Ibsen, 1895, painted by Erik Werenskiold. Note the stern glare of this pillar of society, whose plays scandalized most of his narrow-minded contemporary audiences.

1824 The Maly (the Russian word for 'small') Theatre opens, providing a base for a theatrical company formed in 1806; it is the oldest theatre in Moscow.

1832 Tsar Nicholas I commissions the building of the Alexandrinsky Theatre in St Petersburg; he is credited with virtually inventing the patriotic play, encouraging playwrights to flatter him.

1849 Russian novelist Feodor Dostoyevsky is sentenced to four years' hard labour in Siberia for political crimes. In *The House of the Dead* (1862), he describes the sadism and squalor of the penal colony.

1800~1900

Big Plays by Men with Big Facial Hair

Pushkin, Griboyedov, Gogol, Tolstoy and Chekhov

The poet Alexander PUSHKIN *(1799-1837) had a large beard and wrote few good plays. His best was the romantic* Boris Godunov *(1825, produced in 1870), a tragedy about 'man's fate and the people's destinies'. Nikolai* GOGOL *(1809–52) was a novelist who wrote one superb farce called* The Government Inspector *(1836), about a town duped by its own paranoia. He merely had a moustache.*

Boris Godunov (left) and *The Government Inspector* (above).

Alexander GRIBOYEDOV (1795–1829) had a small beard. *His Woe from Wit* (1824), a brilliant philosophical treatise on how a chap gets victimized and imprisoned in a soulless society (you know the feeling), became the basis for Russian national comedy. *Count Leo Nikolayevich* TOLSTOY (1828–1910) was another novelist, who turned to drama when he was almost 60 (he had to get *War and Peace* and *Anna Karenina* out of the way first, and who could blame him?). His plays were not very good. One of them, *The Light That Shines in Darkness* (1888), concerned a nobleman who wanted to live as Christ but whose wife wouldn't let him ('You're not going into any wilderness, my lad, until that drain's unblocked!). Tolstoy had a huge beard. He ended his days in a shed, having renounced everything except his rampant egomania.

PROMPT BOX

Although the Moscow Arts Theatre takes the spotlight for Russian theatres, there was another theatre that had paved the way, as it were. As early as 1853, the Maly Theatre in Moscow, which premiered Gogol, Ostrovsky and Ibsen in Russia, had rejected French Classical and Romantic influence and embraced Realism.

Throughout this century, Russian acting styles, and the role of director, remained traditional even if more popular. It was left to the best Russian dramatist of them all,

1858-61 Czar Alexander II oversees the emancipation of Russian serfs but they fail to achieve economic independence.

1891 Construction begins on a Trans-Siberian Railway to link Moscow with the Pacific coast.

1899 Prince Volkonsky is appointed Director of the Russian Imperial Theatres; attempting to introduce the ideas of designer Alexandre Benois and choreographer Diaghilev, he falls out with both.

Anton CHEKHOV (1860–1904), in conjunction with Stanislavsky and the Moscow Art Theatre, to bring about a new realistic theatre and 'naturalistic' acting style. They demanded 'natural' responses in actors, so that the inner psychological reactions of their characters to a situation could be more important than the situation itself. Before these men (who both wore neat 'goatee' beards) met, Chekhov's plays had been failures, even jeered off the stage because actors and audiences preferred bellowing voices and windmill arm-waving. It is true to say Chekhov's plays, especially *The Seagull* (1896), *Uncle Vanya* (1897), *The Three Sisters* (1901) and *The Cherry Orchard* (1904), created the need for Stanislavsky's acting experiments, and together they changed the face of Russian theatre.

So there you have it! Big facial hair = small plays; small facial hair = big plays. (Shakespeare, you'll remember, had a small beard, so that definitively proves the theory.)

Supporting Roles

Mikhail Shchepkin, *who had been a serf actor became known as the father of Realism. His pupils included* **Glikeriya Fedotava** *(who was Stanislavsky's tutor),* **Mariya Ermolova**, **Pavel Mochalov** *and* **Prov Sadovsky**, *who all helped earn the Maly the title of 'the second Moscow University'. Schepkin was also responsible during the early part of the century for running the Maly Theatre, known as 'the house of actors'.*

Training Serfs

Empress Catherine II (the Great) 1762–96 wrote terrible plays but encouraged the theatre to be a 'national school'. Through her the Bolshoi Theatre was built in 1771 and an Imperial Theatre training school for actors in 1779. She relieved many nobles from state obligations to start a 'serf' theatre system, where young performers were sponsored (and sometimes beaten) to be great actors.

Looks as though Tolstoy has just singed the end of his beard in a samovar. Painted by Ilya Repin, 1887.

1878 Mr A.A. Shultz, a hairdresser of Auburn, Massachusetts, discovers that the application of hot towels after shaving makes skin healthier and subsequent shaving easier.

1885 Benjamin Keith and Edward Albee acquire a chain of vaudeville theatres in major cities across the United States; only with the rise of cinema and radio will vaudeville lose its popularity.

1890 Thomas Edison advises using 1,000 volts for the first execution by electric chair in New York; the execution is hideously bungled.

1860~1907

Melodrama, Disaster and the Follies!

America after the Civil War

By the Civil War, America, from east to west, had established a strong mainstream tradition of popular drama. And part of that tradition (derived from European models) was a gloriously moralizing and sentimental style of melodrama.

The twin evils of drink and slavery were its main concerns. *Uncle Tom's Cabin*, adapted variously from Harriet Beecher Stowe's novel, is a good example, as is *Shenandoah* (1888) by Bronson Howard, which drew inspiration from the Civil War. The main character in *Rip Van Winkle* provided a money-spinning role for the actor Joseph Jefferson. He co-created the play with one of the best writers of melodramas in America, Irish-born *Dion Boucicault* (1820–1890), who wrote some interesting work, such as *The Colleen Bawn* (1860), *The Octoroon* (1859) and *The Shaughraun* (1874).

PROMPT BOX

Melodrama also embraced the Native American as noble hero and the frontiersman (with wonderfully camp names like 'Nimrod Wildfire') as an enduring symbol of strength and tenacity associated with the West ('a man's gotta do…' etc. etc. – you know the sort of thing). Perhaps one of the best-known such heroes was Davy Crockett, who first appeared in 1872 in the melodrama of the same name by Frank Murdoch.

Frank Mayo became associated with the role of Davy Crockett and played it from 1872 till 1896.

Burlesques (e.g. John Brougham's *Pocahontas;* or, *The Gentle Savage*, 1855) and pantomimes were popular, as were 'spectacle' and 'disaster' theatre with special effects, music and lavish scenery.

Ever wondered where the archetypal idea of tying the flailing heroine to the railway track came from? Well, it was all down to the popular melodramas of one Augustin Daly; *Under the Gaslight* (1867) had a man tied to the tracks (and he was rescued by a woman!); a woman was stranded on a ship about to explode in

1895 Joseph Francis Keaton is nicknamed 'Buster' by Harry Houdini when, as a baby, he survives a fall down a flight of stairs without injury.

1896 Alphonse Mucha's poster for a production of Alfred de Musset's drama *Lorenzaccio* shows French actress Sarah Bernhardt in male attire.

1906 English engineer George Washington, visiting Guatemala, discovers that coffee boiled at high altitude keeps its flavour – his instant coffee will be included in US Army rations.

A Flash of Lightning (1868), and a man was strapped to a log as it entered a sawmill in *The Red Scarf* (1868). All in a day's work.

The great American musical took proper shape from about 1840. After European copies, the first truly American musical was *The Black Crook* of 1866, against which ministers fulminated and raged (which they're so good at). Following such wonderful publicity, it ran for 475 performances and established Niblo's Garden as a top venue. Gilbert and Sullivan premiered in 1879 and positioned comic opera as the dominant musical entertainment.

But, during the 1890s, changes occurred. Victor Herbert wrote the influential comic opera *Prince Ananias* (1894). Then in 1898 two all-black companies wrote and performed *A Trip to Coontown* and *The Origin of the Cakewalk* (the former is unlikely to be revived). As the new century dawned the stage was set for Florenz Ziegfeld's *Follies of 1907* that shifted the emphasis from humour to elaborate scenery, comedians and girls, girls, girls!

Behind the Scenes

Niblo's Theatre, which staged *The Black Crook*, was completely redesigned for the occasion. *The Times* reported that the whole stage could be removed, traps introduced anywhere, and entire scenes sunk into the vast cellar. It included music, a melodrama and a ballet and lasted from 7.45pm to 1.15am. Perhaps that was the real reason why ministers raged against it: it left people too tired to get up in the morning and go to church.

Daly's *Under the Gaslight* where the heroine rescues her lover. The macho film industry reversed the roles.

A Good Egg

The greatest exponent of pantomime was George L. Fox who worked New York's National Theatre as a comedian. He produced *Uncle Tom's Cabin* and staged many pantomimes at the Old Bowery theatre. An expressive mime, he reached his peak in *Humpty Dumpty* (1868), for 1,200 performances, but in 1875 he went mad on stage and was removed to an asylum. Perhaps someone had pointed out to him that he had played Humpty Dumpty 1,200 times.

1875 *Swan Lake* is first performed, unsuccessfully, in Moscow, to music by Tchaikovsky; the score is too sophisticated and subtle for musicians and dancers used to 'hack' ballet music.

1897 The SS *Turbinia* is the first ship to be driven by a steam turbine.

1909 American writer and humourist Ring Lardner joins the staff of the *Chicago Tribune* and is assigned to cover the Cubs baseball team.

1863~1938

From Russia with 'Loved You, Darling!'

Stanislavsky: the father of acting

No name in theatre has dripped more luvvie-ingly from an actor's tongue than that of Konstantin STANISLAVSKY *– alias Sergeevich – (1863–1938). The Russian creator of such thespian catchphrases as the 'magic if' ('What if this character's situation were real?'), 'emotional memory' (using emotive events from one's past to give character motivation – problematic, see page 114) and 'you must live the part' (also problematic i.e. 'But Your Honour – I was preparing for the role of Hannibal Lecter!').*

Danchenko

Danchenko's role in the Moscow Art Theatre has been overshadowed by that of Stanislavsky (mainly because Danchenko wasn't an egotistical actor and didn't write a book called *My Life in Art*, Stanislavsky, 1926). But still it was Danchenko who arranged the historic meeting with Stanislavsky and it was he who lured Chekhov back to theatre and revived *The Seagull*.

Although Stanislavsky wasn't the only person to regard acting as a bit more complex than putting on funny hats and pretending to be someone else, he was the first to systematize actor training. He wanted to make it appear 'real' – i.e. not acting at all (spot the dilemma). Stanislavsky loathed the semaphore acting, commercial star system, predictable plot and tacky-backdrop stage design of the bourgeois Russian theatre. He wasn't too keen on typical audience response either (rowdy would be a good word), since he wanted his actors to imagine a 'fourth wall' between them and the great unwashed (of course, this wall magically disappeared during applause). Despising mere entertainment, Stanislavsky wanted theatre to fulfil a psychologically inspired 'cultural mission', to promote those heady realms of education and good citizenry: fun was definitely off the agenda.

1917 At the end of Tsarist rule, Moscow has 16 of the 250 theatres in Russia; 20 years later, it has 60 of the 560 permanent theatres in the Soviet Union.

1928 Josef Stalin introduces the first Five-Year Plan to collectivize Soviet agriculture; millions of rich peasants are bankrupted or exiled for attempting to resist collectivization.

1934 Grigori Alexandrov directs the Russian film *Jazz Comedy* which complies with the official requirement that films should be understood by all.

PROMPT BOX

Stanislavsky was aware of, but unable to handle, other new directions in drama. He opened a studio for experimental work, but after inviting Meyerhold to produce Maeterlinck's *The Death of Tintagiles* in 1905 he refused to let the play open because he considered the acting to be 'too stylized'. So much for experimentation and concern for the audience: if Stan the Man didn't like it, no one else was given a chance to see it.

Stan the Man trying to recapture emotional moments from his past?

In 1897, he had an 18-hour conversation with playwright *Vladimir Nemirovich-Danchenko* (1858–1943) – I timed it myself – and they decided to collaborate in founding the Moscow Art Theatre. The following year saw his great artistic partnership with playwright Anton Chekhov producing/directing *The Seagull* (1898), *Uncle Vanya* (1899), *The Three Sisters* (1901) and *The Cherry Orchard* (1904). It was struggling with the new 'untheatrical realism' of Chekhov's work, as well as with other avant-garde theatre developments (e.g. Symbolism), the failure of his Studio under Meyerhold, and finally 'sitting on a bench in Finland and examining my artistic past' (1906) that spurred Stanislavsky to formalize an entirely new approach to acting. This 'System', as it became known, was to be the most dominant influence in 20th-century Western theatre performance.

Behind the Scenes

The realistic box sets with their 'imaginary fourth wall' (an idea from Antoine's experiments with the Théâtre-libre) made few compromises to sightlines and visibility. And, although the Moscow Art Theatre used real furniture, props, food and so forth, they also made wide use of painted backdrops and sometimes even two-dimensional painted trees. Well... even big, burly, butch Russian stage-hands didn't fancy lugging trees on and off stage. And I for one wouldn't argue with *them*.

The original 1904 MAT production of *The Cherry Orchard*.

1892 Belgian architect Baron Victor Horta designs his first major work, Tassel House in Brussels; the Art Nouveau interior displays his characteristic whiplash lines on wall decorations, doors and staircases.

1893 French Jews are blamed for the collapse of the Panama Canal Co., whose bankruptcy has cost many French investors their savings.

1900 The *Guide Michelin*, financed by tyre-manufacturers André and Edouard Michelin, is published in Paris, the first systematic evaluation of European restaurants.

1890~1920

Mysticism, Romance and Symbolism

The French and the Russians

Symbolism!

As Realism swept the West, many felt there was a bit more to theatre than boring representations of some idiot's view of 'reality'. In the last decade of the nineteenth century, a movement calling itself 'Symbolism' emerged from France (known for its Big Movements – ask any doctor) to return drama once again to its symbolical and mythical roots.

Taking Wagner and Nietzsche as mentors, subjective Symbolism placed the individual/artist as hero in his own life, in a mystical drama which revealed inner states and where mood and evocation replaced bald statement and linear narrative. Stage managers liked it too; they didn't have to worry about 'authentic' props. But then again, they did have to find 'authentic' audiences.

In 1890 the 18-year-old Paul Fort opened the Théâtre d'Art in Paris, committing it to Symbolism with a production of *The Intruder* (1890) by the Belgian writer *Maurice* MAETERLINCK (1862–1949). The Antoine-trained actor *Aurelian* LUGNÉ-POE (1869–1940) took over the Théâtre d'Art in 1893 and renamed it the Théâtre l'Oeuvre. Fort's house style was stylized/abstract décor, unrealistic intoned dialogue and a dream-like atmosphere, which perfectly suited Maeterlinck's mystical dramas. Acting was also stylized because Maeterlinck originally wrote characters for marionettes (he didn't think much of actors – an attitude shared by other practitioners i.e. Jarry, Craig). Fort also produced *Ubu Roi* by Alfred Jarry in 1896 for just two performances (although he regretted that, see page 106). Not all was radical experiment. In 1897, *Edmond* ROSTAND (1868–1918) saw his

The eloquent Cyrano (he's the one on the right).

1912 Belgian painter and sculptor Rik Wouters completes his bronze *The Mad Virgin*, inspired by American-born dancer Isadora Duncan.

1913 American manufacturer Henry Ford introduces assembly line production, increasing efficiency and reducing costs to make cheaper cars.

1920 Agatha Christie's fictional Belgian detective Hercule Poirot makes his first appearance in *The Mysterious Affair at Styles*.

A drawing of the 1920 staging for Evreinov's *The Storming of the Winter Palace*. This was BIG theatre worthy of a BIG revolution.

PROMPT BOX

Apart from writing *The Inspector General* (1912), which parodied various directors' approaches to Gogol's play, and *The Fourth Wall* (1915), which revealed the stupidity of Stanislavsky's devices in relation to opera (or perhaps the stupidity of opera in relation to Stanislavsky's devices?), Evreinov's greatest achievement was scripting and staging *The Storming of The Winter Palace* (1920), with a cast of 10,000 on Uritsky Square in Petrograd. Everybody works!

work about the poet with the big nose, *Cyrano de Bergerac*, produced.

In Russia the Symbolist poet and dramatist *Alexandr* BLOK (1880–1921) was influenced by popular theatre forms and the mysticism of the philosopher Vladimir Solovyov (as were many other young writers including Bely; see box, right). Blok wrote *The Puppet Play* (1906), rewriting 'commedia' characters as God-seekers and apocalyptic seers (Go for it, Al!). But perhaps the most complete anti-realistic man of the theatre was *Nikolai* EVREINOV (1879–1953). Although not a great writer, he was immensely original. A dramatist-director-theorist and historian, he tried to revitalize theatre by rediscovering it as imaginative play (which preceded arguments about literary value and aesthetics). He wrote *An Introduction to Monodrama* (1909), which sought to define the audience as co-creator and help dissolve the boundary between theatre and life.

Supporting Roles

The first half of **Alexandr Blok***'s life embraced Symbolism and mysticism, the second half a staunch Realism. What caused this change of heart? Partly the failure of the 1905 Revolution, which upset Blok spiritually; but also perhaps the fact that his wife had a glad eye for* **Andrei Bely***, his Symbolist colleague. Blok later called Symbolists 'decadent charlatans'. I wonder why?*

1920 Adolph Levitt founds the Donut Corporation, which markets a doughnut-making machine and ready-prepared mix.

1922 When 40,000 black-shirted Italian Fascists demand strong government, King Victor Emmanuel appoints former schoolmaster and journalist Benito Mussolini, Il Duce, to the post of prime minister.

1924 Bronislava Nijinska's ballet *Les Biches*, with music by Poulenc, is performed for the first time by the Ballets Russes in Monte Carlo.

1920~1940

Illogical and Unreal, but So Happy

The Futurists

Given the overwhelming changes visited upon the Western world from the last decade of the nineteenth century to the end of World War I (including cars, planes, electricity, mass production, psychoanalysis, etc.), it's hardly surprising that art, always in the vanguard of social change, should wrestle with the enormous implications.

Supporting Roles

Bruno Corra *(1892–1976) and* **Emilio Settimelli** *(1891–1954) wrote sketches and plays for live performance. They also contributed to the* Manifesto of Futurist Cinema *in 1916. Futurists were great supporters of film, even making their own (Settimelli appears in one,* Vita Futurista*). In 1910, Corra was the first to paint directly on to film, a technique copied and developed by later artists. These mostly came from wealthy Italian families who didn't know that paper is actually cheaper.*

Marinetti (known in his time as 'the Caffeine of Europe') in a pose suggesting either a certain confidence or starchy trousers. He set the pace for 20th-century theatre.

In *Le Figaro* in February 1909, *Filippo T. Marinetti* (1876–1944) wrote an article entitled 'The Founding and Manifesto of Futurism', following it in 1915 with 'From The Futurist Synthetic Theatre'. In both he called for art to embrace new technology and the spontaneity, dynamism, speed and movement of the machine. 'Get rid of the past,' he cried, 'including all its art galleries, museums, academics, concert halls, "prose" and "musical" theatre, and especially realism and naturalism,' because 'It's

1934 Italy defeats Czechoslovakia at Rome's Stadio Torino, winning the World Cup football competition.

1939 American poet Ezra Pound begins making pro-Fascist broadcasts from Rome to the United States.

1940 Leon Trotsky, a prime mover of the Russian Revolution, dies in hospital in Mexico City; he has been struck in the head with an ice-pick by Ramon Mercader, possibly an agent of Stalin.

PROMPT BOX

Futurism is often associated with Italian Fascism, especially during its 'second' phase. But this connection is spurious since, as explained above, Russian Futurists embraced the diametrically opposed Communist revolution with as much enthusiasm. Marinetti himself, however, was a friend of Mussolini and a great supporter of Fascism. More importantly, Futurism is inherently fascistic in its violent insistence on disregarding everything except its own references.

stupid to write a hundred pages when one will do!' and, 'IT'S STUPID TO RENOUNCE THE DYNAMIC LEAP IN THE VOID OF TOTAL CREATION!' Perhaps I'd better throw those mushrooms away.

Marinetti wanted instead an 'illogical', 'unreal' theatre with poems, readings, paintings, sculptures and performance 'works' all happening simultaneously. The intention was to provoke outrage, which would shake the audience out of its cosy apathy. Enrico Prampolini, a later Futurist, called for a new staging, a 'colourless electromechanical architecture' lit by electricity and coloured glass, machines to produce abstractions and an actor who was reduced to a robotic-like function. The Futurists set up about 500 of their 'syntheses' (compressed dramatic examples of Futurist theatre), but hardly any were performed. A second phase of the group's activities came in the 1930s, but by then it had become even more weak and amateurish and was little more than a posing avant-garde.

News of their activities extended to Russia where the brilliant *Vladimir MAYAKOVSKY* (1893–1930) proclaimed himself a Futurist and the 'loud-mouthed Zoroaster of his age. His plays, including *Vladimir Mayakovsky, A Tragedy* (1913), and *Mystery-Bouffe* (1918), embody his preoccupations with time and its effects on personality (his own). His major works, *The Bedbug* (1929) and *The Bath-House* (1930), were grotesque satires sharply criticizing the Communist bureaucracy and parodying the future Soviet utopia. It is thought that their lukewarm reception contributed to his suicide.

Mayakovsy looking as though he's just read the reviews of *The Bedbug*.

Behind the Scenes

Many a director has shrieked 'Get Rid Of Those Actors!' But Enrico Prampolini, second-generation Futurist and innovative theatre designer, director, painter and sculptor, tried to dispense with them permanently. In the *Machine Art Manifesto* (1923), he argued that properly built mechanical scenery with elevators, lighting, phonograph recordings etc. would do a far better job than any bunch of actors. Many years later his dream would come true with many of London's West End hit musicals.

1850 *La Dame aux camélias* by Alexandre Dumas *fils* is performed for the first time; the play is an early example of French social drama.

1872-3 Monsieur Marcel, *le roi de l'ondulation*, invents the Marcel Wave; ten years later, he can afford to retire.

1902 Vsevolod Meyerhold founds the Society of New Drama in Russia; he eliminates scenery and treats the actor as a puppet in the hands of the director.

1850~1922

Take Your Pick. We Got Naturalism...

Hauptmann, Gorky, O'Neill

Since Tom Robertson put real bread and tea on stage in 1860 (see pages 74–5) academics have got their knickers in a twist (normal dress code for many of them) in defining 'Naturalism' and 'Realism' and what, exactly, is the difference between them.

Maxim Gorky photographed in 1900, looking down but not out.

Although, in both, action arises from character, logic from sentiments, and plot from plain old life (working-class was de rigeur), Realism is a style, a 'real-seemingness', in a performance where, despite the apparent reality of the proceedings, it is no more 'real' than any other artistic form you may care to mention. Naturalism is much the same except it is claimed there is a greater depth to the relationship between character and environment (which is usually one of utter misery). Raymond Williams, in *English Drama: Forms and Development* (1977), said 'Naturalistic' characters' lives 'soaked into their environment...and the environment...soaked into the lives'. There you are: is that all clear now?

Anyway, Naturalism plugged the gap created by the general 19th-century subject matter of the 'classical' stage and 'real' lives of ordinary people. In Germany, *Gerhart HAUPTMANN* (1862–1946) wrote *The Weavers* (1892), a major Naturalist drama of 'the workers', where the crowd is

Behind the Scenes

Naturalism has made thespians do the silliest things to maintain the illusion of the 'fourth wall': such as actors facing the audience and 'warming' their hands at an invisible fire; or the mirror on the back wall painted to look like it 's reflecting wallpaper and not the audience. It was a sad day when audiences stopped throwing things at the stage, considering what some actors chuck at audiences.

1902 French novelist and polemicist Emile Zola dies of asphyxiation from carbon monoxide fumes due to a blocked chimney.

1908 The First International Congress of Psychoanalysis is held in Salzburg; Freud, Brill, Adler and Jung attend.

1919 In protest against the Treaty of Versailles, Rear-Admiral von Reuter orders seamen to scuttle the entire German fleet in the harbour at Scapa Flow in the Orkney Islands.

Laurence Olivier and Dorothy Cummings in *Long Day's Journey into Night* at the National Theatre.

Supporting Roles

Among other 'classics' of Naturalism are The Happy Family *(1890), a German play by* **Arno Holz** *and* **Johannes Schlaf** *about a family that was anything but, and the boring English mining plays of D.H. Lawrence. Today, television soap operas are Naturalism par excellence, and it seems that some poor souls even send birthday presents to fictional characters. Proof, I think, that the human race is doomed.*

the hero. In Russia, *Maksim* GORKY (*Alexei* PESHKOV, 1868–1936) wrote *The Lower Depths* (1902), an angry and sympathetic view of down-and-outs. Gorky was not a happy man in any event; even his *nom de plume* meant 'Maksim The Bitter'. In America, *Eugene O'*NEILL (1888–1953), who claimed Strindberg as his mentor, tried living in the 'lower depths' for a while. His best contributions to Naturalism were his 'sea plays', *Bound East for Cardiff*, *In the Zone*, *The Long Voyage Home* and the *Moon of the Caribbees* (all 1914–18), although he wrote in several genres.

The main problem with Naturalism is the obvious one of compromising the artifice of theatre, which is at its heart. Novelty devices like real tea, food, grass (yes, I've actually caught hay fever inside a theatre before now) etc. reduce theatre's primary source of power, the imagination. Additionally, Naturalism has meant that stage design has been governed not by creative expression, but by one of the 20th-century obsessions, namely 'authenticity'.

Eugene O'Neill and Agnes Boulton on the verandah of their house in Massachusetts.

1856 French novelist Gustave Flaubert's *Madame Bovary* is declared an immoral novel; both he and his publisher are prosecuted.

1889 Painter Carl Larsson returns from Paris to Sweden; his paintings of idealized everyday life, using clear, transparent colours will influence interior design.

1901 In reprisal for his repression of student agitators, the Russian propaganda minister is assassinated.

1850~1950

... Or We Got Realism

Europe and the States

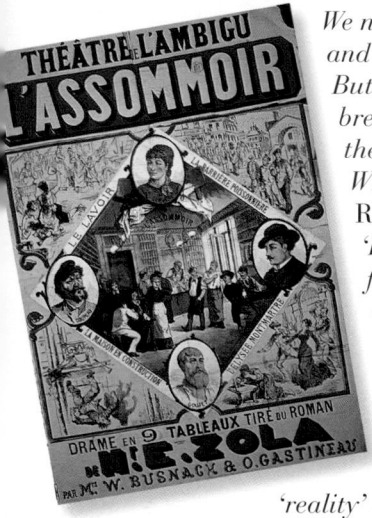

Zola's *L'Assommoir* (1877) is set in the taverns of Paris.

We now understand that 'Realism' is itself a style and no closer to reality than any other art form. But in 19th-century Europe it represented a breakthrough in displacing the Romantic theatre, which had become very predictable. When Emile Zola dramatized his novel Thérèse Raquin *in 1873 (probably the first truly 'Realist' play), it was claimed theatre was finally representing the 'reality' of unheroic ordinary lives on stage. But Zola's drama was very dull and literal in its slavish adherence to things 'natural'. It was left to later writers, like Ibsen, Strindberg and Chekhov, to show what the theatre really needed – not 'reality' but the impression of reality. Realism not only redefined the structure and style of a production, but also consolidated something else: as an orchestra needs the conductor, theatre now found that it needed the director.*

Strindberg and his daughters, 1884: digging himself a place in history.

I have already mentioned European 'Realist' directors such as Saxe-Meinengen, Antoine, Stanislavsky etc. because that is where the impulse began. But by the end of the century Realism was also entering the American mainstream alongside vaudeville,

1913 Unknown to each other, T.S. Eliot and e.e. cummings appear in a Harvard production of *Fanny and the Servant Problem*.

1929 350,000,000 handkerchiefs are sold in the United States.

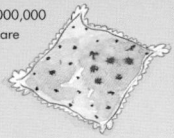

1946 At Nuremberg, in Germany, the Leaders of the Third Reich are tried as war criminals; Joachim von Ribbentrop and Hermann Goering are sentenced to death but the latter kills himself.

melodrama and the spectacular. *David* BELASCO (1853–1931), a writer of (forgettable) realistic plays, is best remembered for the pioneering and meticulous realism of his essentially melodramatic productions (even transferring real buildings to the stage). The designer *Norman* BEL GEDDES (1893–1958) was probably most famous for being the 'father of streamlining' in industrial design and some brilliant Symbolist theatre designs (i.e. *The Miracle*, 1923). But he also designed very realistic sets, including *Dead End* (1935).

Behind the Scenes
When Stanislavsky staged Andreyev's *The Life of Man*, he covered the stage in black velvet and put on it 'sets' of rope, a different colour for each act. Actors also wore black costumes with rope outlines. Although it was successful, Stan was unhappy. 'I do not feel the actors have moved forward,' he said. Perhaps they couldn't see, Stan.

Taking the Moscow Art Theatre as their model, in 1931 a group of artists including Lee Strasberg (who formulated method acting – see page 114), Harold Clurman and Cheryl Crawford began an experiment called the Group Theatre, as a platform for new American plays of social significance. Actually they engendered more good actors (i.e. John Garfield, Morris Carnovsky, Franchot Tone) than writers, although one, the brilliant and Chekhovian *Clifford* ODETS (1906–63), gave the Group its voice as he transformed working-class life into poetry with works such as *Waiting for Lefty*, *Awake and Sing!* and *Paradise Lost*, all premiering in 1935.

Peter Gowen and Janet McTeer in a scene from Ibsen's *A Doll's House*. No doubt the letter contained some 'real' words.

PROMPT BOX

Realism is the dominant mode of dramatic representation in film and television. Film is able to use other forms, such as Expressionism, Surrealism and, of course, spectacle. Television mostly uses Realism or Naturalism, with occasional tame forays into other forms (i.e. game shows and the like).

Suffering for Art
To challenge his actors in a production of Hauptmann's *The Sunken Bell*, Stanislavsky dangerously broke up the surface of the stage. 'Let them creep... (and) sit on stones. Let them descend into the trap and climb out again,' he said. This would 'force them to get used to a new mise-en-scène'. Today's actors would respond: 'Let me phone my union, my lawyer... .'

1907 Australian swimmer Annette Hellerman is arrested on a Boston beach for wearing a one-piece swimsuit without a skirt.

1914 John Singer Sargent's portrait of Henry James is mutilated by a suffragette on the first day of its exhibition in London.

1916 Eugene O'Neill's *Before Breakfast* is staged in Greenwich Village; the author plays a character whose only utterance is a gurgle as he slashes his throat with a razor.

1907~1925

Or If It's Been a Bad Hair Day...

How about Expressionism?

Expressionism as a concept sprang from painting, and has been used to mean every kind of non-realism imaginable, including Surrealism. Unlike Realism, which represents how external 'reality' affects the artist, 'Expressionism' describes how an artist imposes their own concept of reality on the outside world by expressing their own emotional experience (which is fine unless the artist is barking mad). Or something like that.

Supporting Roles

The Son *(1917), by* **Walter Hasenclever** *(1890–1940), was a key Expressionist work;* Heaven and Earth *(1920), by* **Paul Kornfeld** *(1889–1942) marked a high point for Expressionist theatre. Originally a 'Naturalist',* **Leopold Jessner** *(1878–1945) turned Shakespeare's* Richard III *into an Expressionist play. There were also* **Reinhard Sorge** *(1892–1916), a so-called 'ecstatic' Expressionist,* **Reinhard Goering** *(1887–1936),* **Arnolt Bronnen** *(1895–1959) and* **Otto Falckenberg** *(1873–1947).*

Like all movements, Expressionism has its forerunners, in this case Strindberg and *Frank* WEDEKIND (1864–1918). Wedekind's plays departed from Naturalism in their episodic structure and grotesque caricatures as characters. His first major work, *Spring's Awakening* (1901), did not get performed until 1906 because of its radical form and shocking theme (adolescent sex. Quite right too! Everyone knows girls and boys don't until

Toller wrote *The Machine Wreckers* while in prison for advocating Communism.

1920 The Bloody Mary cocktail is invented by a bartender at Harry's New York Bar in Paris.

1923 Maidenform brassières are introduced to give girls a bit of an uplift.

1924 Adolf Hitler is convicted of high treason and sentenced to five years in prison, where he starts writing *Mein Kampf* (*My Struggle*).

Oscar Kokoschka checking there's nothing Expressionist up his sleeve.

they're 21!). The 'Lulu' plays, *Earth Spirit* (1895) and *Pandora's Box* (1904), also depict a society obsessed by lust and greed. So what else is new?

Oscar KOKOSCHKA (1886–1980), apart from having a name that sounds like someone sneezing, was a highly influential painter and dramatist who provided some of the earliest examples of Expressionism. His *Sphinx and Strawman* (1907) was one of the most impressive theatrical excursions into the subconscious and influenced the later Dadaist theatre (see page 106). Two names most associated with German Expressionism are *Ernst* TOLLER (1893–1939) and *Georg* KAISER (1878–1945). Toller's *Masses and Man* (1920) and *The Machine Wreckers* (1922) depict strike action and Luddite attacks by worker/slaves on factories. Kaiser, in *From Morn to Midnight* (1917), created a modern Morality play which took a lowly clerk on a distorted, dream-like and episodic journey for spiritual enlightenment. Expressionist theatre travelled to America where Eugene O'Neill (see page 95) wrote two great Expressionist plays, *The Emperor Jones* (1920) and *The Hairy Ape* (1921), which caused the critic, John Willett, to call him the best Expressionist dramatist of all.

Britain, as always, wasn't tolerating any damn silly foreign ideas, so anyone attempting to import one had to leave it at Passport Control and collect it on the way out. And the sooner the better!

Cabaret

Frank Wedekind sang rude ditties in the infamous 'Die elf Scharfrichter' ('The Eleven Executioners') club in Munich. Cabaret was then a popular entertainment across Europe. Clubs called 'Black Cat' (Paris), 'Noise and Smoke' (Munich), 'Four Cats' (Barcelona), 'The Bat' (Moscow) all served a 'menu' of salacious poems, music and sketches. It is rumoured Wedekind was once ejected for urinating on the audience. They didn't find it too funny, strangely enough.

PROMPT BOX

Ernst Toller was a passionately political man who founded a militant-pacifist group. He became president of the first short-lived Bavarian Soviet Republic in 1918 and later commander of its Red Army. Then he spent five years in prison when the 'Republic' fell in 1919. He committed suicide as World War II broke out.

1892 The first lavatories are provided on British trains; hitherto, ladies travelling on long journeys (in segregated carriages) have had to bring their own chamber pots.

1902 British novelist and essayist Samuel Butler dies; at his own request, his ashes are buried anonymously in the crematorium garden.

1905 The New York production of George Bernard Shaw's *Mrs. Warren's Profession* is closed by the police because it is an 'immoral' play; the first London production is in 1926.

1890~1915

Jewels in the Dross

Irony and fantasy in England

While Europe and America were having so much fun with Expressionism and cabaret etc., what were English thesps up to? Being dull and pompous, that's what. In late Victorian and Edwardian England most 'serious' theatrical output was dire and, like everything else in that era, obsessively snobbish and class-divisive.

Poster showing G.B. Shaw as a Russian demon king.

Poster for Harley Granville-Barker's production of *The Taming of the Shrew* at the Royal Court Theatre.

Music hall (constantly under attack from a puffed-up self-righteous middle class), despite odd flashes of genius, all too often descended into self-parody, whilst melodrama, the regular fare of the theatres, was mawkishly sentimental and moralizing. Spectacular shows blossomed at the Hippodrome and Coliseum, but they were little more than novelties produced by men who would do anything to make money (rather like those in the West End and Broadway over the last 30 years).

However, a few rose above the dross, and they mainly came from Ireland. Actor, playwright, director and critic *Harley Granville-Barker* (1877–1946), a major influence on British theatre, took over the Royal Court in 1904 and bravely initiated new work, including 11 plays by *George Bernard Shaw* (1856–1950) (this was brave in itself!). The Irish-born Shaw wrote endlessly and influentially about everything. His plays, trademarked by ironic and witty iconoclasm, were often confrontational – such as *Widowers' Houses* (1892), about slum landlords and *Mrs Warren's Profession* (1902), about prostitution. The later *John Bull's Other*

1909 Robert E. Peary claims to be the first person to reach the North Pole; later research suggests he got his sums wrong and was actually between 30 and 60 miles away.

1910 The first exhibition of post-impressionists is held at London's Grafton Gallery, with work by Van Gogh, Cézanne, and Matisse.

1914 German and British soldiers declare a truce on Christmas day; they play football and exchange gifts before resuming hostilities the next day.

Supporting Roles

The melodramas of **Henry Jones** *(1851–1929), such as* Saints and Sinners *(1884), and* The Case of Rebellious Susan *(1894), although successful, revealed a timidity in criticizing the stifling contemporary moral values.* **Arthur Wing Pinero** *(1855–1934) also chose not to stick his neck out too far.* The Second Mrs Tanqueray *(1893) ends obsequiously when his heroine commits suicide just because she doesn't fit in.*

Island (1904), was Shaw's first successful play in London; it grappled with that vexing 'Irish question', which, as we all know, is still being grappled with now.

Oscar WILDE (1854–1900), also an Irishman, had more drama in his life than his plays. His intention was to satirize, ruthlessly, the dull and pompous melodrama that was the order of the day, but, nevertheless, even his best work, *The Importance of Being Ernest* (1895), was, like all his plays, drama not theatre. That is, though witty and socially pertinent, the plot contrivances are weak and the staging unadventurous. Publicity about his homosexuality, and the court trials that followed, closed the play and put him in prison. He was declared bankrupt, spent his last years wandering around Europe and died in Paris.

Other names to note include the novelist *John* GALSWORTHY (1867–1933), who wrote *The Silver Box* (1906), *Strife* (1909) and *Justice* (1910), all produced by Granville-Barker and dealing with social and moral themes. *J.M.* BARRIE (1860–1937), author of *Peter Pan* (1904), *The Admirable Crichton* (1902) and *Quality Street* (1902), injected a note of well-crafted escapist fantasy (if a little over-romantic and whimsical) into otherwise social dramas.

An 1884 Oscar Wilde caricature captures the contemptuous expression.

Behind the Scenes

The Hippodrome (built in 1900 as a circus) had a large water tank for aquatic spectacles (no, not swimming goggles). In 1910 it premièred Tchaikovsky's *Swan Lake* (literally!). The Coliseum (1904) was the first music hall in England to possess a revolving stage. A venue for Diaghilev's Ballet Russes and ice shows, in 1968 it became the home of the English National Opera.

Water ballet at the Hippodrome.

1900 John Millington Synge, working as a literary critic in Paris, makes a third trip to the Aran Islands; W.B. Yeats has advised him to go there and 'express a life that has never found expression'.

1901 James Joyce, an undergraduate at Dublin University, attacks the proposed National Theatre for Ireland in a two-penny pamphlet called 'The Day of Rabblement'.

1917 Mata Hari, an exotic dancer known for her scanty costumes and love of feathers, is executed as a spy.

1899~1940

Of Playboys and Gunmen

The Irish connection

J.M. Synge painted by Jack Butler Yeats. Behind those calm, steady eyes, an angry man fumed at the Church and the English state.

It takes more than 300 years of English repression of Gaelic culture to stop the Irish being a very literary and poetic people (as the customers of any Irish pub will tell you – endlessly). So it's no surprise that in 1897, W.B. YEATS (1865–1939), along with Lady Augusta GREGORY (1852–1932), formed the 'Irish Literary Society' in Dublin to help de-Anglicize the arts and effectively start a long overdue Irish national theatre.

Inspired by Lady Gregory's translations of Irish heroic legends, Yeats wrote romantic heroic verse dramas like *The Countess Cathleen* (1899). Joining forces with the amateur Irish National Dramatic Society, who had produced *The Shadow of the Glen* by the then unknown Irish writer J.M. Synge, they became in 1904 the Irish National Theatre Society, which then became the Abbey Theatre (later giving none other than Orson Welles his first acting job). *J[ohn] M[illington] SYNGE* (1871–1909) had lived in Paris and the Aran Islands. This gave him material for his best work, *Riders to the Sea* (1904), *The Tinker's Wedding* (its

Annie Horniman

Ironically the profits of English colonialism financed the Irish National Theatre. In 1894 Annie Horniman inherited her father's tea fortune and began financing the activities of Yeats' enterprise, including the Abbey Theatre (1904). In 1907 disagreements forced her to leave. She then set up the first English repertory company in Manchester. They had their opening season at the Midland Hotel Theatre.

1918 The 'Shingle' style of short hair for women will be followed in 1931 by the Mingle and the Cringle.

1926 When the audience riots at a performance of Sean O'Casey's *The Plough and the Stars* at the Abbey Theatre in Dublin, W.B. Yeats tells them, 'You have disgraced yourselves again.'

1939 Dublin-born poet, dramatist and Senator of the Irish Free State, W.B. Yeats dies and is buried in France; after the war, his body is transferred to the Drumcliffe Churchyard in County Sligo.

anti-clerical tone so frightened the Abbey, let alone the Church, it wasn't produced until 1971), and most famously *The Playboy of the Western World*, which caused riots in 1907. Although he used realistic sets and props, he elevated peasant speech to dramatic poetic rhetoric. His settings might be workers' cottages, but his characters were wild and fantastic, like Christy, an outcast artist 'Playboy' with attitude.

Yeats and the Abbey stuck with the proscenium arch and box set until the 1950s, letting the language dominate the work. This is especially true of plays by *Sean O'Casey* (1880–1964). At first his political themes were realistically set, as in *The Shadow of a Gunman* (1923), which dealt with the Anglo-Irish war before the 1921 settlement; *Juno and the Paycock* (1924), set after the settlement during the Civil War; and *The Plough and the Stars* (1926), a version of the 1916 uprising. But he experimented, and when he offered *The Silver Tassie* (1928), which included Expressionist ideas, the Abbey refused it. O'Casey was outraged, broke contact with them, and departed for England.

Supporting Roles

Padraic Colum *(1881–1972), member of the Irish National Theatre Society; wrote* Broken Soil *(1903) and* The Land *(1905).* **William Boyle** *(1853–1923) with* The Building Fund *(1905), and* **T.C. Murray** *(1873–1959) in* Birthright *(1910), continued the tradition of Realist Irish writers. The brilliant fantasy plays of* **George Fitzmaurice** *(1877–1963), like* The Pie-Dish *(1908), marked a welcome exception.*

PROMPT BOX

Synge's comedy, *The Playboy of the Western World*, which somewhat challenged the unquestionable purity of Irish morals, upset more than a self-righteous Dublin audience. On its opening night in New York in 1911, Irish-Americans also rioted. But ex-President Theodore Roosevelt, who attended the opening, gave a glowing appraisal of both play and players to the press, which silenced most opposition.

An unholy Irish row erupts in O'Casey's *The Plough and the Stars*.

1871 Over 19 per cent of men and 26 per cent of women in Britain can not sign the parish register when they marry; by 1891, the percentage will drop to about 7 per cent.

1881 The Duke of Saxe-Meiningen's Meiningen Players perform at Drury Lane Theatre in London; the use of split-staging, crowd choreography and the conception of a production as a whole are revolutionary.

1895 The first game of professional football is played in the United States.

1849~1935

A Shutter in the Dark

Craig, Appia, Wagner, Constructivism

Two of the most influential 'visionaries' in Western theatre were the Englishman (Edward) Gordon CRAIG *(1872–1966) and the Swiss, Adolphe* APPIA *(1862–1928). In* The Art of the Theatre *(1905), Craig called for a non-naturalistic 'director's' theatre which would appeal to the emotions through movement alone.*

Gordon Craig's set for *Macbeth*, 1928, must have made the actors somewhat nervous.

He was full of plans to sweep away boring realism and the dominance of 'words' but, like those of most visionaries, his ideas couldn't be built. His 30-metre high shutters, to be moved by 'invisible' means, or his fluid architectural shapes to be created during a performance, were parts of what he called 'scene'; everyone else called them 'impossible'. (One wonders if he developed theories as to the breeding of a superhuman stagecrew.)

Collapsing Hamlet

Stanislavsky invited Craig to design and direct *Hamlet* in 1912. Craig wanted huge screens built out of metal. Stanislavsky said that was too heavy, so Craig suggested the Moscow Arts Theatre be rebuilt! They compromised on canvas and wood (giving us our modern 'flats'). After two years of preparation the play opened, but two hours before curtain up, the whole lot collapsed.

Appia emphasized the power of focused electric light (still in its infancy) to 'colour' moods and create mystery or symbolism. By writing 'scores' for lights, just as choreographers did for dance, he gave the world the lighting 'plot' (which in turn unfortunately gave us that bizarre sub-species, the lighting technician). Nowadays he could probably have got a job working for Pink Floyd.

PROMPT BOX

Craig wanted to do away with the actor (which one he didn't say). 'The actor is for me only an insuperable difficulty and expense,' he said. He declared that an 'übermarionette', or super puppet, totally manipulated by the 'puppeteer' (the director, of course) would be the best actor. I think there are a few out there now, Gordon.

1903 Researchers working for German coffee importer Ludwig Roselius invent a process to remove caffeine from the beans; the result is Sanka (sans caffeine).

1907 American novelist Theodore Dreiser becomes editor of *Butterick Publications*; he manages to slip in poems between the dress patterns and advice to the Jenny Wren Club.

1927 American dancer and sometime lover of Edward Gordon Craig, Isadora Duncan dies in a racing car, strangled by her long scarf.

The gate for such ideas had been opened by the Gesamtkunstwerk, or 'total artwork' idea of Richard Wagner (see page 77) based on the (then radical) notion that all elements in a production should be unified. He had a theatre built at Bayreuth in 1876 to demonstrate his theory (those were the days!). Gesamtkunstwerk would, he claimed, provide a 'communal experience' for performers and audience. However, another of his bright ideas, the darkening of the auditorium during the performance, changed all future theatre beyond recognition. From that moment, the fundamental sense of unity and social interaction between audience and players, essential to theatre from the earliest rituals, was gone. Audiences were psychologically 'shut out' from events on stage; they became voyeurs. (Let's face it, sitting in the dark watching others is in any circumstances a questionable thing to do!) So much for a 'communal experience'!

In Russia, Lyubov Popova, Vladimir Tatlin and others declared 'Constructivism' as the design aesthetic of the machine age. Like the Expressionists and Futurists, they saw design as a combination of abstract vision and the laws of mechanics. Vsevolod Meyerhold, the brilliant director, utilized Constructivist theory for both actor training and staging (see page 108).

Supporting Roles

Max Reinhardt *(1873–1943), one of the first directors (after Saxe-Meinengen), became famous for encouraging new acting techniques and scenic design (he used the revolving stage – an idea originally pinched from the Japanese), although his productions were always illusionistic. Most associated with the Deutsches Theatre, Berlin (until the Nazis arrived), he later worked at Salzburg, Vienna and America.*

Behind the Scenes
Wagner's Bayreuth theatre (1876) dispensed with things like boxes, pit, galleries etc. in favour of 'democratic' seating such as we are now used to. The auditorium contained 30 rows of seats which were arranged in a fan shape, doubling in width from front to back, and with aisles on either side instead of in the centre.

For the production of Wagner's *Valkyrie* in Paris in 1893, they used lights and a cyclorama screen to make the horse-riding scenes realistic.

1896 In Germany, Karl Lautenschlüger introduces the first revolving stage.

1903 Arthur Conan Doyle agrees to bring Sherlock Holmes back from the dead and is paid $5,000 each for at least six stories.

1904 Charles Rolls and Henry Royce become partners in a new car-making business.

1896~1930

Mad People and Modernists

From Dada to Ubu

Perhaps the craziest movement of all was Dada, started by Tristan TZARA *(1886–1963), Hugo* BALL *(1886–1927) and others, at the Cabaret Voltaire, Zurich, 1914. Not exactly a 'theatre' movement, it nevertheless used performance as a weapon. And what a weapon it turned out to be!*

Jarry's grotesque, self-important Père Ubu is captured in his friend Joan Miro's Surrealist painting. Ubu symbolized the greed of bourgeois society.

Bourgeois audiences were invited to soirées only to have abuse, irony, satire, bombastic 'art' declarations and sometimes furniture hurled at them! They even did it in the streets and frightened the horses. Initially a reaction to World War I, it preshadows the Existentialists, the 1960s 'Happenings' and the punk aesthetic, as a signifier of the trademark sense of chaos, cynicism and brutality of the 20th century. A more formally political version of Dada appeared in Berlin in 1916.

A hero of Tzara's was *Alfred* JARRY (1873–1907), the creator of one of the most important and devastatingly prophetic portrayals of despotism, Père Ubu, in his Shakespearian parody, *Ubu Roi* (1896). *Ubu* played only twice, riots closed the theatre, but has remained an icon of anarchist theatre.

War Protests

The Berlin Dada activities were aimed specifically at German involvement in the War. At the first 'exhibition' of performance, sculpture and painting, the cartoonist George Grosz dressed some pig carcasses in the uniform of the Kaiser's troops and hung them from the ceiling. He was in prison before he could say 'That's Dada volks!'

1912 On its maiden voyage from Southampton to New York, the S.S. *Titanic* strikes an iceberg and sinks.

1917 French composer Erik Satie's ballet *Parade* is performed with décor by Pablo Picasso and libretto by Jean Cocteau.

1926 German film-maker Fritz Lang and his scriptwriter wife Thea von Harbou make *Metropolis*, a film about a futuristic city state.

Several 'modernist' writers, although seemingly more mainstream, were influenced by Dadaist thinking. *Federico García* LORCA (1898–1936) and *Luigi* PIRANDELLO (1867–1936) experimented with many styles, including Surrealism, fantasy and farce. Lorca is mostly remembered for his passionate peasant trilogy *Blood Wedding* (1933), *Yerma* (1934) and *The House of Bernarda Alba* (1936). But he also wrote *The Prodigious Shoemaker's Wife* (1926), a puppet-like farce, and *As Five Years Pass By* (1929), a Surrealist play within the mind of a man about to die. Lorca was murdered by Spanish Falangists at the age of 38.

PROMPT BOX

Jarry was 15 when he wrote *Ubu Roi*. He intended it for puppets, and even when it reached the stage he wanted actors to be 'puppet-like'. Later he wrote three other 'Ubu' plays before virtually becoming Ubu, riding around Paris on a bicycle with pistols strapped to his belt. He drank himself to death at 34. I blame the parents (and the bartenders).

Learn your lines

Jarry's views on audiences: 'There are... at least two: that of the intelligent, small in number, and that of large number... .'

And on theatre: Two things are '... notoriously horrid... and... encumber the stage uselessly:.. the scenery and the actors.'

He wanted mere placards to state location, and actors wearing masks and using monotone voices. Had they ever met, he and Craig would have got on well.

Pirandello was a sceptical pessimist (his wife was barking mad) and obsessed with the relationship between (fixed) art and (fluid) life. His best known work, *Six Characters in Search of an Author* (1921), initially caused uproar. But we now see it as a seminal modernist attack on traditional theatre and bourgeois European values. You know the sort of thing.

Oscar SCHLEMMER (1888–1943), a German sculptor and director of the Bauhaus Theatre, attempted to design theatre from an abstract point of view, using costumes in geometric shapes to create 'moving architecture'. His ideas were realized in the Triadic Ballet, 1912–22, where dancers were attired in geometrically shaped costumes – and looked interesting, if a little silly.

Schlemmer's Triadic Ballet characters were defined according to his theories of shapes and colours.

1917 Lenin hates smoking and bans all cigarettes from the train that takes him to Petrograd to initiate the Bolshevik Revolution.

1921 France makes abortion illegal to compensate for all the population lost during the Great War.

1931 Alfred M. Butts invents 'Criss-Cross', a game played with wooden tiles on a board. James Brunot will take it over, name it Scrabble – and win.

1917~1939

Experiments Between Lenin and Hitler

Meyerhold, Piscator, Brecht

In the early twentieth century, Europe overflowed with new forms and approaches to that old business of mincing about in funny clothes. No, I'm not talking about the armed forces or the Church (or their off-duty attire), but theatre, dahlings, theatre!

Behind the Scenes
Technical innovations should never be an end in themselves, said Piscator. Stage design should 'elevate the events on the stage onto a historical plane', and not just enlarge the technical range of machinery. 'This elevation... [is]... inextricably bound up with the use of Marxist dialectics', and 'my... devices... [are]... developed to cover up the deficiencies of the dramatists' products...' (ouch!).

In Russia the genius *Vsevolod* MEYERHOLD (1874–1940) explored several styles of theatre, all with extraordinary effect. At the Moscow Art Theatre, in 1905, Stanislavsky put him in charge of his new Studio and invited him to experiment with non-naturalistic forms. Influenced by oriental theatre, Meyerhold, like Craig, believed that the essence of theatre lay in movement and its difference to reality, not an imitation of it. Stan didn't like this at all, so Meyerhold went elsewhere and, under the pseudonym 'Dr Dapertutto', explored commedia dell'arte, circus, pantomime and puppets. After Lenin, he moved on to revolutionary theatre and Constructivism, trained his actors in the science of biomechanics, and finally explored socialist realism. But, from being one of the most revered artists in Russia, he fell foul of Stalinist thinking and was murdered in 1940 (his wife was butchered, too). Joe was never too much of an art lover.

Meyerhold's set for *Tarelkin's Death*, 1922: a 'machine for acting'.

1936 Salvador Dali appears at the opening of a Surrealist exhibition in London wearing a scuba-diving suit.

1937 Nazi bombers under orders from General Franco destroy the Basque town of Guernica.

1938 The British use 651 million gallons of water per day; by 1979 it will be 5,000 million gallons a day.

One of the most significant creative forces in Germany was *Erwin* PISCATOR (1893–1966). He developed a kind of political agit-prop style which incorporated film, photography, recorded voice and live action into a montage theatre. His revealing of the means of production (all the backstage stuff normally concealed by the proscenium arch) denied illusion. Overall, his trail-blazing in what came to be called epic theatre (see box below) influenced Brecht, with whom he collaborated to produce *Rasputin* in 1927.

Bertholt BRECHT (1898–1956) became the most influential writer/director in the West since World War II. His theories, as much as his plays, have created a template for non-illusionist political theatre, especially 'alienation', that much-abused term (see box). His many texts, including the Expressionist *Baal* (1919), *The Threepenny Opera* (1928), *The Life of Galileo* (1938), *Mother Courage* (1939) and, perhaps his best, *The Caucasian Chalk Circle* (1948), are revived endlessly. To escape the Nazis he fled to America, but left in 1948 to escape McCarthyism and established the Berliner Ensemble theatre with his wife, the actress Hélène Weigel.

The Caucasian Chalk Circle performed at the National Theatre in 1997.

Alienation

The 'alienation effect' or, to use the German, Verfremdungseffekt, was Brecht's way of stopping actors from identifying with their roles, and demonstrating them instead. He used devices to distance the audience, such as having the actors whisper asides or wear strange masks. The technique, known as 'epic theatre', thus relied on audiences' reflective skills to interpret the action. Brechtophile directors, eager to copy the master, made this device something of a thespian buzzword. It wouldn't have gone down at all well with Method actors.

1926 Recuperating from an addiction to opium, French dramatist, film director, artist and poet Jean Cocteau writes his tragedy *Orphée*.

1935 The employer of Carson McCullers, disturbed to find her reading Proust during office hours, dismisses her summarily.

1940 Imprisoned for entering Britain without a visa, Arthur Koestler 'would mark Pentonville with three stars. It is the most decent jail I have been in'.

1925~1970

Happiness is... a Good Thrashing

The ecstasy and cruelty of Artaud and Grotowsky

Whatever else they may be, visionaries tend not to be very practical. In The Jet of Blood *by the Frenchman Antonin* ARTAUD *(1896–1948), one stage direction calls for the genuine Hand of God to appear! I bet that pleased the stage manager. And one wonders how the acting of God affected their insurance policies.*

Antonin Artaud in *The Passion of Saint Joan*, 1928. The eyes say it all.

An uncompromising man, Artaud founded the Théâtre Alfred Jarry (see page 106) in 1927, having been thrown out of the Surrealist movement for being too extreme (get the picture?). His notion of theatre as an act of cruelty (which became infamous in London during the 1960s via Charles Marowitz's 'Theatre of Cruelty' season) was a huge influence on European and American avant-garde theatre. He didn't mean physical cruelty to the actors (unfortunately) but a spectacle of violence and sexuality to offend the audience out of their complacency. In 1938 he codified these thoughts in a seminal work, *The Theatre and Its Double*, where the 'double' of theatre was real life. To him, what was needed to combat the word-dominated rhetorical theatre was a 'poetry of space' filled with music, dance, painting, chanting

How Not to Act

Jerzy Grotowsky said acting was '... a process of self-revelation, going back as far as the subconscious', and the construction of a score 'whose notes are... what we call "give and take". We... do not teach him [sic] how to create [for example, how to play Hamlet] ... for it is... in this 'how' that the seeds of banality and... clichés that defy creation are planted'. Food for thought, don't you think?

Behind the Scenes

From Artaud's *Theatre of Cruelty Manifesto* (1932): 'We intend to do away with the stage and auditorium, replacing them with a... single, undivided locale without any partitions of any kind... Direct contact will be established between... actors and audience'. Theatre architecture should be a 'barn or hangar' like 'some churches, holy places, or certain Tibetan temples'.

1951 The American government carries out above-ground nuclear tests in the Nevada desert; hundreds of square miles are contaminated.

1958 In Ethiopia, locusts consume a million pounds' worth of grain.

1970 American rock-blues singer Janis Joplin dies of a heroin overdose at the age of 27; she is one of the first white singers to achieve success with the blues.

Supporting Roles

Artaud founded the Théâtre Alfred Jarry with **Roger Vitrac** *(1899–1952), a Dadaist who wrote at least one excellent Surrealist play,* Victor *or* Power to the Children *(1928). This was a satire with a grotesque nine-year-old protagonist (he was six-foot tall, for a start!) who was able to see straight through the pretensions and hypocrisy of bourgeois values and patriotism. Vitrac's subsequent plays were flops and he gave up theatre. Oh, the fickleness of the paying, theatre-going public!*

and gesture. He envisaged a model for theatre based on 'a police raid on brothels'; 'theatre was to be like the plague from which people would emerge either dead or purged'. Predictably, most of his later years were spent in an asylum.

In Poland, at his Theatre of 13 Rows (in Opole) and later in his Teatr Laboritorium, *Jerzy* GROTOWSKY (1933–1999) trained his actors to enter a trance state wherein it is rumoured some could slow their own heartbeat and produce welts on the skin during mimed flagellation scenes. Influenced by Artaud, he also wanted a radical theatre of poetry, which would transform the actor-audience relationship. His was a 'poor' theatre without make-up, costume, décor, stage, lights and sound effects: the only necessary elements were 'an actor and a spectator'. (However, every single production he did, including Goethe's *Faust*, Mickiewicz's *Forefather's Eve* and Wyspiansky's *Acropolis* carried production credits for direction, costume, properties and design. Hmm!)

Grotowsky outside his Teatr Laboritorium in 1966.

Grotowsky's major work, *Towards a Poor Theatre*, was as thorough a guide to acting as were the writings of Stanislavsky – it just didn't catch on quite so well. Perhaps he overlooked the fact that people generally go to the theatre to enjoy themselves.

Peter Brook's *Marat/Sade*, 1964: his turn to do some Theatre of Cruelty.

1944 Anne Frank's family are betrayed to the Gestapo after more than two years in hiding.

1947 Buckminster Fuller develops the geodesic dome. He will develop geodesics, the mathematical study of economical space-spanning structures.

1950 The body of a man ritually murdered in about 240 BC is discovered in a peat-bog in Denmark; Professor P.V. Glob's *The Bog People* investigates this and other similar grisly finds.

1944~1961

Meanwhile, in Life's Waiting Room

Existentialism

Existentialism, or 'heroic pessimism', is a philosophy that developed in France after World War II as a response to a meaningless world in which freedom of choice is denied. Since each person is thus a 'free agent' trying to control his or her life, personal experience and responsibility are all-important.

Alec McCowan and John Alderton in *Waiting for Godot* at the National Theatre. Just hanging around.

Its archpriest was *Jean-Paul Sartre* (1905–80), who, in plays like *The Flies* (1943) and *No Exit* (1944), attempted to invent a 'theatre of situations' where actions define characters rather than any psychological state. *Albert Camus* (1913–60), another Existentialist, wrote *Caligula* (1945), and *The Just* (1949). Frankly, both wrote better novels and essays. Their plays were mostly longwinded public debates.

Possibly the greatest writer and thinker to emerge this century was the Irishman, *Samuel Beckett* (1906–89). What Sartre and Camus couldn't resolve theatrically, Beckett did with consummate brilliance.

Beckett's principal works, from *Waiting for Godot* (1955) to *Happy Days* (1961), superbly depict that ol' sense of futility in short metaphorical images of bleak clowning, despair, depersonalization and the desperately comic struggle to 'keep things going' no matter what, whilst waiting for something to happen (Ain't it just so?). Instead of endless discussion, his scenarios are stripped to the bone in word

PROMPT BOX

Beckett's love of music hall is evident in his characters and their situations. The comedian's sense of desperation to keep going to the bitter end, no matter what the audience response, is echoed by Beckett's characters as they wait, struggle to remember, or try to find purpose in their existence. It's as if he sees the clown's act as a metaphor for all our lives.

1949 French philosopher, essayist, novelist and partner of Jean-Paul Sartre, Simone de Beauvoir publishes her feminist essay *Le Deuxième sexe (The Second Sex)*.

1955 The millionth Volkswagen 'beetle' rolls off the production line.

1961 Soviet Cosmonaut Yuri Gagarin is the first human in space; in a flight lasting only two hours, his tiny space capsule circles the earth at a maximum altitude of 187 miles.

(some are silent), deed (sometimes characters literally do nothing) and setting (they are located 'nowhere', with a minimalist set). They are, somehow, magically, also superb theatre.

Camus once described human existence as 'absurd', which helped the critic, Martin Esslin, title his book, *The Theatre of the Absurd* (1961). One of its inclusions was the half-French, half-Rumanian *Eugène Ionesco* (b. 1912), whose first play, *The Bald Prima Donna* (1950), was inspired by reading English phrase books. With story and characterization replaced by surreal and hallucinatory events, it perfectly mirrors the crazy world we live in. Subsequent one-act plays, *The Lesson* (1951), *The Chairs* (1952) and *Rhinoceros* (1960) placed him as one of France's top theatre writing talents. They are successful, possibly because they don't forget to be funny.

Behind the Scenes
During World War II many European theatres were destroyed. Germany began to rebuild and produce immediately (they also improvised with some of the huge stages of the old opera buildings). In Britain, old theatres fell into decline, but the rise of the Arts Council funded a growing repertory movement. In America, the new university provided regional centres for theatre.

Supporting Roles

Jean Genet *(1910–86), poet, novelist and playwright, made his name writing homoerotic novels whilst in prison. He revolutionized theatre with five plays including* The Maids *(1947),* The Balcony *(1956) and* The Blacks *(1959). Highly theatrical, his plays reveal the abuses of power, and suggest that all social roles exist partly to deceive.*

William Sabatier, Jean-Louis Barrault and Simone Velere in *Rhinoceros*, 1960.

1954 Ray Kroc visits Mac and Dick MacDonald's hamburger stand in San Bernardino California; his chain of fast food restaurants based on their model will earn him $600,000,000.

1955 American drama critic Walter Kerr publishes *How Not to Write a Play;* 'the fun-loving American finds the theater infinitely resistible – and at any price.'

1959 Glen Raven Mills of Altamahaw, N.C. introduce pantyhose – waist-high nylon tights requiring no additional support.

1947~1990s

The American Method

(Or how I stopped acting and learnt to mumble)

Life membership in the American club.

In 1947, Elia Kazan and others from the Group Theatre (see below) founded a workshop called the Actors' Studio. It charged no fees, was not a school, and anyone who got past the tough audition was a member for life. Since then, everyone who is anyone in American theatre and film has been a member, from Marlon Brando to Ellen Burstyn and Dustin Hoffman. In 1963 the Studio opened its own theatre on Broadway, although this closed shortly after.

When Group member *Lee STRASBERG* (1901–82) took over artistic direction in 1951, the Studio became home to a 'shrug and mumble' school of acting known as the Method. Founded on the least interesting part of Stanislavsky's work (the bit that goes on about psychology and the actor's 'emotional memory' – see page 88), the Method unforgivably persuaded actors that what they feel is basically all that matters (and they don't need much encouragement to think that!). In so doing, it elevated the actor to undeserved heights of neurotic self-importance whilst lowering acting to equally undeserved depths of self-indulgent mannerism.

Lee Strasberg offering tips on Method acting.

Supporting Roles

Cheryl Crawford *(1902–86) co-founded the Group Theatre, and later the Actors' Studio. Always seen as the steadying influence within the Group, she kept the peace between Clurman and Strasberg (whom she referred to as 'Old Testament prophets'). After she left the Group she independently produced musicals, such as* Brigadoon *(1947) and* Paint Your Wagon *(1950), as well as plays.*

1961 About 1,500 Cuban exiles, backed by the CIA, fail in their attempt to overthrow the Cuban president, Fidel Castro; the Bay of Pigs fiasco further sours Cuba's relationship with the USA.

1995 32-year-old American film director Quentin Tarantino's *Pulp Fiction* is a heady blend of violence, comedy and gloss.

1997 Boxing star Mike Tyson, convicted of rape in 1992, bites off a chunk of opponent Evander Holyfield's ear; Tyson is disqualified and Holyfield's ear repaired by surgery.

Brando oozing testosterone and mastication in *Streetcar*. Note the 'realistically grubby', though painted, setting.

In 1934, when the brilliant actor, teacher and Group member Stella Adler returned from working with Stanislavsky in Paris to pass on his reaffirmation of 'character' as essential to dramatic action (and thus acting as essentially a pretence), Strasberg metaphorically put his fingers in his ears and sang loudly. Nevertheless, the Method went on to become the quintessential style in 20th-century American theatre and (especially) in Realist film.

The director, *Elia KAZAN* (b. 1909), produced new American Realist plays and films of, for example, *A Streetcar Named Desire* (1947), *Death of a Salesman* (1949) and *Cat on a Hot Tin Roof* (1955) in a highly naturalistic 'Method' style, full of intense feelings, emotions and brooding sexuality (most of which were put there by the playwrights).

Liz Taylor plots how to seduce her husband in *Cat on a Hot Tin Roof*.

PROMPT BOX

Of the actors associated with the Method, Marlon Brando (b. 1924) is the most famous. His first notable appearance was in Elia Kazan's stage production of *Streetcar*. Dustin Hoffman (b. 1937) carried on the tradition in *Death of a Salesman* as did Ellen Burstyn in *Same Time, Next Year* (1975). The rest, as they say, is history.

1925 Irish playwright George Bernard Shaw is awarded the Nobel Prize for Literature but refuses to accept it, for political reasons.

1932 Typographic consultant Stanley Morison's new typeface, 'Times New Roman' gives Britain's longest-running newspaper, *The Times*, a more contemporary look.

1937 Shirley Temple and her American studio receive damages of $9,800 after British novelist Graham Greene suggests in an article that her older male fans find the little star's appearance titillating.

1925~1956

Stiff Upper Lip, Crease in your Flannels

(Or a creased upper lip and a stiff in your flannels?)

The period between the wars and up to the 'watershed' year of 1956 (when Look Back in Anger *was performed, see page 120) was a kind of theatrical playtime in England. Having had little contact with Expressionism, Dada, Futurism etc. (but aware of them), and in contrast to any politically motivated revolutionary or post-revolutionary European theatre, English drama focused on social comedies, farces or mildly controversial 'Realist' plays about social ills or World War II. Naturalism and traditional 19th-century staging dominated and Shaw was still King, of course.*

Coward's plays could hardly be called innovative.

Noel trips the light fantastic with Gertrude Lawrence in *Private Lives*.

Noel COWARD (1899–1973) was known as 'The Master' in theatrical circles (but Master of what?). His plays, from *Fallen Angels* (1925), through *Hay Fever* (1925), *Private Lives* (1930) to *This Happy Breed* (1942) and the even worse *Peace in Our Time* (1947), were at best slight, brittle comedies of bourgeois manners and at worst rather nauseating patriotism. His was a reactionary, flag-waving world where the rich were jolly fine people and the poor had the decency to know their place. The 1920s weren't called frivolous for nothing! Coward also wrote some ditties and tunes and was awarded a knighthood in 1970.

Terence RATTIGAN (1911–77) was another writer of weightless comedies, such as *French without Tears* (1936). He got a bit serious with *Flare Path* (1942), about his wartime experiences, and dipped a toe

1939 King George VI and Queen Elizabeth, on a visit to Canada and the United States, eat hot dogs with President and Mrs Franklin Roosevelt.

1954-5 English philologist and specialist in Old Norse language and literature J.R.R. Tolkien publishes his fantasy trilogy, *The Lord of the Rings*, which will achieve cult status.

1956 British anti-nuclear protesters march from the Aldermaston research station to London.

Supporting Roles

There were some exceptions to the theatre of 'toffs' and 'gels'. **Joan Littlewood** *(b. 1914) and* **Ewan MacColl** *(1915–89) founded the experimental, left-wing Theatre Union in 1935, which paved the way for the agit-prop theatres of the 1960s. Influenced by German political theatre, Littlewood directed many controversial plays and pioneered the medium of documentary drama. Her most famous production was* Oh, What a Lovely War! *(1963).*

into social realism with *The Winslow Boy* (1946), about a miscarriage of justice. His most well known play is *Separate Tables* (1954), a study of the psychological impact of cravat and flannels on a tweed two-piece suit. He was knighted in 1971.

Separate Tables: a tale of emotional inadequacy in a seaside hotel.

R[obert].C[edric]. SHERRIFF (1896–1975) wrote several plays but only *Journey's End* (1928), an angry and realistic portrayal of soldiers at the front line, was any good. Shaw called it 'a useful corrective to the romantic conception of war'. The farceur, *Ben* TRAVERS (1886–1980) had ten of his comedies put on at the Aldwych Theatre from 1925 to 1933. These became known as the 'Aldwych farces', and included *A Cuckoo in the Nest* (1925), *Rookery Nook* (1926) and *Dirty Work* (1932). His last farce, *The Bed before Yesterday*, was written and staged when he was 89 years old.

Behind the Scenes

Of course, the biggest crowd-puller of the time was the 'talking-pictures', and the wireless was very popular too. Music hall still had some life in it via Max Miller, George Robey and Gracie Fields, but television finally nailed it into its coffin. Live entertainment now lives on in comedy and variety shows, and in rock concerts.

1937 American pioneering aviator Amelia Earhart and her plane, the Flying Laboratory, set off to fly around the world; they disappear over the Pacific Ocean.

1938 Austrian psychoanalyst Sigmund Freud, 82, takes refuge from Nazi Austria and moves to London.

1945 Dissatisfaction with commercial theatre leads Joan Littlewood and others to found the Theatre Workshop; from 1953, the company will be based at the Theatre Royal at Stratford in London.

1930~1970

Keep One's Vowels Regular!

Gielgud, Richardson, Olivier

Who needs Russian Constructivism, Italian Surrealism, German Expressionism, Piscator, Brecht or even the American 'Method' when it's perfectly obvious that real theatre only needs a bit of aristocratic elegance and perfect diction? If American acting was 'shrug and mumble', in England it became all 'head and voice', where nothing moved from the neck down.

PROMPT BOX

Donald Wolfit (1902–68), the last actor-manager, loved to give really good value for money. He spent many years touring 'classical' roles, and one of his best was as Oedipus in *Oedipus Rex*. Ever the showman, he would shock and delight audiences when Oedipus 'put out his eyes' by staggering from the wings with two peeled red grapes sliding down his face.

And to those philistines who complain that such acting is anti-theatrical, stultifyingly dull, and has the physically expressive range of a wooden plank, or that a pretentiously aristocratic English accent that ignores the richness of the regions, not to mention Scotland, Ireland or Wales, reduces theatre to a snobbish, elitist pastime, the only response is a contemptuous gaze, flared nostrils and a single arched eyebrow. How dare they! For what can be more spiritually uplifting or theatrically exciting than a fencepost spellbinding us with mellifluous, rounded tones? (What? I say, steady on, old man!)

Sir John GIELGUD (b. 1904) began knocking audiences off their plush seats in 1924 as Trofimov in *The Cherry Orchard*. He has gone on to ever-greater things at the Old Vic and just about every major theatre since. His most famous role is that of Hamlet, which he produced himself in 1933 and, apart from championing Shakespeare, he has helped make Chekhov agreeable to the English by producing adaptations of his plays.

Ralph RICHARDSON (1902–83) was better made for contemporary

Sir John Gielgud's Hamlet (1934), looking more fed up than royally troubled.

1949 English journalist, essayist and novelist George Orwell publishes *Nineteen Eighty-Four*, a chilling futuristic fable of totalitarianism.

1963 John Gielgud: 'Good verse-speaking is rather like swimming. If you surrender to the water it keeps you up, but if you fight you drown.'

1968 Billie Jean King is the first American woman in 28 years to win all major tennis competitions in Britain and the United States.

Olivier as Archie Rice (1957) captures in his rictus the desperation of fading music hall.

Supporting Roles

Actors **Paul Scofield** *(b. 1922)* **Emlyn Williams** *(1905–87)*, **Charles Laughton** *(1899–1962) and* **Michael Redgrave** *(1908–85) all developed their talents in either the Old Vic or Stratford. Directors, too, like* **Tyrone Guthrie** *(1900–71), and foreign imports* **Michel Saint-Denis** *(1897–1971) and* **Fyodor Komissarzhevsky** *(1882–1954) helped the Vic become one of the most important theatres in England.*

plays than Shakespeare. He excelled in 'ordinary' parts where he could display his natural sense of gentle innocence and fair play. Plays by Somerset Maugham and J.B. Priestley, especially the latter's *Johnson Over Jordan* (1939), were perfect. Later in his illustrious career he specialized in playing a selection of rather eccentric bumblers in theatre and film.

In 1970, *Laurence* OLIVIER (1907–89), was the first actor ever to be made a Lord (what next? President?...oh yes, I forgot). A Shakespearean actor, he also played contemporary parts, such as Archie Rice in John Osborne's *The Entertainer* (1957). He was a film actor and the first director of the English National Theatre in 1963. His physical agility, a 'just get on with it' approach to acting and rather eccentric diction separated him somewhat from his peers. His response to Dustin Hoffman's aggressive Method preparation for his role in *Marathon Man* is classic: 'But dear boy, why don't you just *act* it?'

Dame It!

Edith Evans (1888–1976), Peggy Ashcroft (1907–91), Flora Robson (1902–84) and Joan Plowright (b. 1929) were fellow performers of the boys mentioned above. Joan Plowright married Olivier in 1961. The other three became Dames (no, not in pantomime), and Peggy had a theatre in Croydon named after her (a somewhat backhanded compliment).

Dame Flora Robson (in 1935), mistress of the level stare that was not to be tangled with.

1956 Despite having had no formal coach and training for only one hour a day, 25-year-old medical student from Oxford University Roger Bannister breaks the running record of four minutes to the mile.

1959 *One Way Pendulum* by English playwright N.F. Simpson is a rare example in Britain of the Theatre of the Absurd.

1962 Decca Records turns down the opportunity to sign up the Beatles in favour of a recording deal with Brian Poole and the Tremeloes.

1956~1970

Reviving the Corpse

Osborne, Devine, Wesker, Ayckbourn

On a soap box.

The year 1956 has been called a watershed for British theatre, mainly because the play Look Back in Anger, *by John* OSBORNE *(1929–94), seemed to signal a revival in English drama (which was almost flatlining!). Whilst this is true, it certainly overrates Osborne's play, which centres on Jimmy Porter, a working-class university-educated boy whose rants against middle-class society led to the phrase 'angry young man' (subsequently applied to any artist critical of society). But Porter's anger is more a whine, and he is as reactionary as those he attacks, guilty of material jealousy and weak misogyny.*

PROMPT BOX

Brecht's influence got through to Britain by the 1960s. Joan Littlewood had, of course, noticed it long before, but she was very special. In 1960, the writer Robert Bolt (b. 1924) created *A Man for All Seasons*, starring Paul Scofield. In this he used the 'Brechtian' devices of a narrator and an episodic structure.

Two angry young men: John Osborne (right) with Ken Hough, who played the original Jimmy Porter in *Look Back in Anger*, at the Royal Court, 1956.

More important was the vision of *George* DEVINE (1910–65) whose English Stage Company (formed 1954) produced Osborne's plays at the Royal Court Theatre, and was committed to changing the conditions of theatre in England by new work. Devine helped many new writers and actors find their feet (it's an old theatrical problem – not knowing where your feet are).

One of those writers was *Arnold* WESKER (b. 1932), who, although critically attacked, has often shown more bravery and adventure in his writing than many others and, unlike Osborne, was one of the

1963 The jawbone of *Zinjanthropus*, a man-like creature who lived over two million years ago, is found at Lake Natron in Tanzania.

1969 British troops are sent into Northern Ireland after Protestant-Catholic riots; only in 1998 does the political situation allow the possibility of their permanent withdrawal.

1970 British poet Ted Hughes publishes *Crow*, a sequence of poems with illustrations by Leonard Baskin; its darkness and bleakness will influence subsequent British poetry.

A 1997 production of Wesker's *Chips with Everything* at the Lyttelton Theatre. Class clashes in the RAF.

few genuine working-class writers. Wesker's early works, such as *Roots* (1959) and *Chips with Everything* (1962), helped articulate the working-class socialist hopes that followed the war.

The incredible popularity of *Alan AYCKBOURN* (b. 1939) guaranteed academic and critical indifference for years, for it is a very English (if tiresome and stupid) intellectual snobbery to equate success with poor quality. And successful he is, outstripped in terms of international translations and popularity only by Shakespeare. His plays premièred at Scarborough because, as he sensibly says, theatre is 'like bingo, just somewhere to go when it's raining' (if rather more expensive than bingo). From *Relatively Speaking* (1967) onwards, his plays demonstrate technical acrobatics with incredibly sharp observations of the middle class, using comedy to illuminate the small, if frighteningly claustrophobic, tragedies of life. The *Norman Conquests* trilogy (1974) shows simultaneous events in the dining room, living room and garden of a house one weekend. Theatrically he taps into that modern sense of futile absurdity first articulated by Sartre and Camus – only with jokes.

Behind the Scenes

Ayckbourn's method for writing plays is a lesson in how to get on with it! To avoid facing the 'tyranny of the blank page' for too long, he creates an annual programme for his Steven Joseph Theatre in Scarborough to include a new Ayckbourn play, titled, but not yet written! He then has to write it before the season starts! But one still wonders if he procrastinates to the very last minute... .

Looking for the muse.

Supporting Roles

John Arden *(b. 1930), famous for* Sergeant Musgrave's Dance *(1959), and* Live Like Pigs *(1957), now lives in Ireland and prefers to write for non-professional theatres.* **Ann Jellicoe** *(b. 1927) whose* The Sport of My Mad Mother *(1956) explored non-literary speech rhythms, went on to write* The Knack *(1961). She has long been a supporter of community drama.*

1954 Food rationing ends in Britain and ration books are burned at Conservative Associations right across the country.

1960 A small family-run shoe manufacturer in rural England introduces a chunky, eyelet-laced utility boot with a cushioned sole called 'Dr Martens' after their German inventor, Dr Klaus Maertens.

1963 In Britain, an armed gang hijacks a train (which is carrying bank notes for incineration) and escapes with more than £2.5 million.

1954~1973

Angry Young Persons

The revolutionaries

While Jimmy Porter ranted, other writers in Europe and America were demonstrating a more focused and real anger, though not always politically motivated, and preparing the ground for the 1960's arts 'revolutions'.

Supporting Roles

Shelagh Delaney *(b. 1939) wrote the great* A Taste of Honey *(1958), when she was 17.* Saved *(1965), by* **Edward Bond** *(b. 1934), brought British stage censorship crashing down. The controversial scene of a baby being stoned in a pram was his angry attempt to reflect the moral mayhem of contemporary life. Bond claimed: 'I write about violence as Jane Austen wrote about manners. Violence shapes and obsesses our society... '*

Harold PINTER (b. 1930) was influenced by Beckett. His early work, like *The Birthday Party* (1958), revealed a similar interest in the terror of torment without reason, and *The Caretaker* (1960) has much in common with Beckett's *Waiting for Godot* in its use of a tramp to signify pointless existence (or to signify that life was all about the struggle to get to Sidcup). For years he put 'silence' and 'non-communication' on stage in a big way but, after *Betrayal* (1978), he seems to have changed his style to a more straightforward kind of storytelling.

Joe ORTON (1933–67) rejoiced in defacing library books, promiscuity and brilliant, bizarre and very funny plays with camp dialogue. From *Entertaining Mr Sloane* (1964), he theatrically said the unsayable. His funniest play, *What the Butler Saw* (1969), works as a farce, a Wildean comedy, and a satire of psychiatry. Sadly, he was murdered by his talentless and jealous lover, Kenneth Halliwell, who then committed suicide.

A wide-eyed Joe Orton watching a rehearsal of *Entertaining Mr Sloane*, Wyndham Theatre, 1964.

1964 When Joe Orton's *Entertaining Mr Sloane* transfers to a theatre in London's West End, it is attacked both for being highbrow and a commercial success.

1968 Soviet tanks roll into the Czech capital, putting an end to the economic and political reforms introduced by Alexander Dubcek; the 'Prague Spring' is over.

1973 German-born British economist E.F. Schumacher's *Small is beautiful*: 'Man is small, and, therefore, small is beautiful. To go for giantism is to go for self-destruction'.

The brilliant Leonard Rossiter in Orton's *Loot* (1965), which premiered in Brighton.

Dario Fo (b. 1926), once an established writer/comedian in cabaret, television and mildly satiric plays, realized with horror during the 1960s that his plays were enjoyed by those he sought to pillory. So with his wife, Franca Rame, he formed his own company, Nuova Scena, and later, La Commune, to revive genuine working-class theatre exposing corruption and oppression. Since going for the jugular he has become famous internationally as a comic mime and writer with plays like *Accidental Death of an Anarchist* (1970) and *Mistero Buffo* (1967), explorations of corrupt ideology and human weakness.

Borstal Boy

Brendan Behan (1923–64), an IRA member who had served time in prison, was made famous by Joan Littlewood when she produced his comic account of a prisoner waiting to hang in *The Quare Fellow* (1956). *Borstal Boy* (1958) documented his own time behind bars. He belonged to the same tradition as Sean O'Casey, but unfortunately drank himself to death at the age of 41.

The Afro-American *Amiri BARAKA* (born Leroi Jones, 1934) became a leader of the 1960s black arts political movement. His plays, for example, *Dutchman* (1964), *The Slave* (1964) or *Slave Ship* (1967), display his 'fierce and blazing talent' and strong anti-white feeling. He has had a great influence on black American theatre.

Out of the post-war Women's Liberation Movement came a 'Feminist theatre' fighting sexism in society. Always radical, in most cases their art was suffocated by their self-righteous politics, but some groups successfully channelled agit-prop anger beyond the hectoring phase into sophisticated theatre. An injection of humour is usually all it takes.

Angry black theatre generation meets angry black film generation: Amiri Baraka (centre) and Spike Lee, director of the movie *Malcolm X* (right).

1947 The radio quiz show *You Bet Your Life* has Groucho Marx ad-libbing interviews with guests; translated to the small screen in 1951, it wins an Emmy Award as the funniest show on TV.

1955 Disneyland, the amusement park that is also a holiday destination, opens its doors and proves to be Walt Disney's greatest success.

1956 Arthur Miller is subpoenaed to appear before the House Committee on Un-American Activities; he refuses to implicate other communist writers and is fined for contempt.

1935~1985

Tellin' It Like It Is

The American Realists

One by one the Big Boys emerged with a new style of theatre that wasn't afraid to get its hands dirty. In the politically turbulent American 1930s, Langston HUGHES' Mulatta *put black issues by black writers and actors firmly on the stage. Tennessee* WILLIAMS' *steamy* A Glass Menagerie *premiered in 1945, and Arthur* MILLER'S *keynote* Death of a Salesman *in 1947.*

Purveyor of social protest in poetry: Langston Hughes in 1967, the year of his death.

The Glass Menagerie by *Tennesse* WILLIAMS (1911–83) brought the tensions, heat and suffocation of those poor souls who need booze'n'sex to cope (most people I know, actually) to an astonished and homophobic post-war stage. Two years later his genius was confirmed by *A Streetcar Named Desire*, featuring a glowering, sweaty Marlon Brando as Stanley Kowalski. Williams went on to write some of the finest lyrical theatre ever produced in America in plays like *Cat on a Hot Tin Roof* (1955) and *Suddenly Last Summer* (1958), before declining in power and control. He was, apparently, overfond of intravenous amphetamines and casual sex – two activities one might have thought to be mutually exclusive, but not, apparently, in his case.

How to make a torn vest sexy. Brando fuelling his angst in *Streetcar*.

Behind the Scenes

Film was taking over in America in a big way. Talkies arrived in 1927, with the offensive *Jazz Singer*. Theatres declined by two-thirds in the 1920s as houses built screens, and Manhattan became the centre for professional theatre. Before the Depression, there were almost 300 shows on Broadway; ten years later there were only 80.

1965 Government health warnings on cigarette packets are required by law in the United States.

1973 Richard Nixon, in Disney World, denies involvement in the 'Watergate Affair' and tells the American people that their President 'is not a crook'.

1977 Elvis Presley, the king of rock 'n' roll, is found dead at his Memphis home; rumours of sightings of the King will abound for many years to come.

Supporting Roles

Neil Simon *(b. 1927) is probably the most successful playwright on Broadway. His output (almost a hit a year since 1961) and productions rival Ayckbourn in England. But critical acclaim doesn't come easy. He writes gags well and mild satires of middle-class mores, but his scalpel is not as sharp as Ayckbourn's, nor does it cut as deep. He remains, however, the master of the twinkle and the wry smile.*

Arthur MILLER (b. 1915) won the Pulitzer Prize with *Death of a Salesman*. Although basically a Realist play, it often shifted into Expressionist mode in telling the story of a failed commercial traveller. In 1953 he wrote *The Crucible*, ostensibly about the Salem witch trials, but actually responding to McCarthy's zealous 'subversives' witch-hunt. Since the death of Williams, Miller has been called America's greatest living playwright.

Perhaps the most obscure American playwright is *Sam* SHEPARD (b. 1943). His output of over 40 plays reveals wide and diverse influences like rock and roll, drug culture and dance, and he seems obsessed by myths of the West, the American Dream and notions of 'roots' (in other words, a typical American writer). From *The Rock Garden* (1964), to the brilliant *Fool for Love* (1979) and *True West* (1980), he has stretched the boundaries of the Realist form to accommodate cinematic and graphic art sensibilities.

Male bonding (with balls). Warren Mitchell as Willie Loman in *Death of a Salesman*.

David MAMET (b. 1947) emerged in the 1970s with plays like *Sexual Perversity in Chicago* (a great name to get attention for your first play). In 1977, his *American Buffalo* proved him a writer of great characterization and naturalistic dialogue. *Glengarry Glen Ross* (1983) won the Pulitzer Prize for its tales of troubled Chicago real estate agents (and you must admit it takes real genius to make anyone care about estate agents).

1960 Joseph Beuys produces his sculpture *Bathtub*, the tub he used to bathe in as a child, covered in sticking plaster and soaked in gauze.

1966 The American TV channel NBC premiers the science fiction series *Star Trek* which will continue for 78 episodes and win cult status.

1969 400,000 young people attend a weekend pop festival near the artists' colony of Woodstock in the USA to hear 32 rock and folk groups.

1960~1975

It's the Sixties! So Get Your Kit Off!

Hair and Happenings

Getting into *The Brig*.

The 1960s were the time to 'drop out' from a materialistic world, and change it for the better through drugs, sex and good old rock'n'roll. Embarrassing though it may seem now, it was all rather serious then. And perhaps you may be forgiven for secretly thinking it was rather a good idea.

In England, the same day as the Lord Chancellor's work ended as theatre censor, the nude musical extravaganza *Hair* had its English premiere. Its impact was huge, but it was very much a product of its time. The script was terrible and, as Charles Marowitz commented, there was a certain 'hippie mindlessness' beneath its surface. It was basically just an excuse for the actors to get their kit off in public.

Hair was a commercial version of another experiment: the Happening. The term was coined by the painter Allan Kaprow (sort of originator), and is an event of calculated impermanence and spontaneity. A happening occurs once only and there is no beginning, middle or end. In a happening there is no separation between actor and audience, no script and much is left to chance (just like life, eh?).

Hair had been restaged from an original show by Tom O'Horgan from La Mama

The Woosters

A very influential theatre was the Performance Group (now the Wooster Group) from New York. Under Richard Schechner, they produced *Dionysus in 69*, a total audience participation show (very 1960s) where everyone was asked to join in sexual activities with the cast and each other. Nice work if you can get it.

1971 'Hot pants' become fashionable.

1973 The longest solar eclipse in history is visible from the Southern Sahara desert.

1974 A Swedish woman sues the Israeli psychic Uri Geller, known to TV audiences for his spoon-bending skills, for making her contraceptive loop ineffective.

Experimental Theatre Club (Café La Mama). Started by Ellen Stewart in 1962, La Mama became one of the most important American venues for new work, hosting Grotowski, Peter Brook, Eugenio Barba and others. La Mama was itself influenced by the eclectic activities of Julian Beck and Judith Malina and their Living Theatre (which kicked off the Off-off Broadway theatres). Formed as a collective (which means no one does the dishes), theirs was a confrontational theatre, often shouting in the faces of their audience about various social crimes (like, er... trying to leave the theatre?). Influenced by Artaud, they saw themselves as 'gurus' of a new American pacifist order. (But, hey, Americans believe in the power of complaining!).

Hair also spawned imitators, including *Oh Calcutta* (1969), written by critic Kenneth Tynan (whose fame rested largely on being the very first person to say 'fuck' on television. One wonders who will ever be the last?). He persuaded famous names (including John Lennon, Sam Shepard, Joe Orton and even Sam Beckett) to write bits of pornography as part of the script, while retaining their anonymity. But it was not a success critically, and at least one female critic complained that the male 'members' in the cast remained disappointingly unaroused! Honestly, some people really insist on getting their money's worth at the theatre.

The 1967 production of *Hair* with cast looking like rejects from Village People auditions.

Supporting Roles

Joseph Chaikin *(b. 1935) worked with the Living Theatre in the early 1960s and founded The Open Theatre in 1964 as an experimental company. His approach was workshop-based, wherein actors continually tried new means of extending their art and improvising their dialogue and actions. He has directed many other theatres since, and his influence on modern American acting has been considerable.*

PROMPT BOX

The Living Theatre ran into trouble for non-payment of taxes to the American IRS. The IRS closed their theatre down in 1963 during a run of Kenneth Brown's *The Brig*. The last audiences had to climb in through the windows of the theatre to see it (which no doubt guaranteed a good audience response: who would want to admit that such an effort had not been worthwhile?). After this the Living Theatre exiled themselves in Europe before returning in 1968.

1960 The world's first felt-tip pen is produced by a Japanese company.

1963 President John F. Kennedy is assassinated in Dallas, Texas; Lee Harvey Oswald is subsequently arrested but is himself shot before being tried for the murder.

1965 Unwilling to share power with Rhodesia's black citizens, Prime Minister Ian Smith signs the Unilateral Declaration of Independence from Great Britain.

1960~1979

The Times, They Are A'Changin'

Agit-prop in the UK

If aesthetic change was one side of the 1960s' 'revolutionary coin', political change was the other. Agit-prop (plays trying to initiate political action by agitation and propaganda – basically, yelling at everyone) became a common term; if you weren't a tub-thumping radical, you were a square.

Feeling agitated.

Spurning traditional theatre, small groups of amateurs set up shop in halls and clubs, including the 'fringes' of the annual (and 'high culture') Edinburgh festival. (Or were they just saving face, as traditional theatre spurned them?) Typical of such political groups was Portable Theatre in Brighton, from which *David* HARE (b. 1947) and *Howard* BRENTON (b. 1942) emerged. They wrote *Brassneck* (1973) together, and many other works separately. Hare later moved to the establishment at the National ('Grow up and sell out,' as Lenny Bruce once said.)

John MCGRATH (b. 1935) set up 7:84 Theatre in 1971 (so called because 7 per cent of the population then owned more than 80 per cent of the wealth) as a company for his own plays like *The Cheviot, The Stag* and *The Black, Black Oil* (1973). McGrath tried to revive a socialist and popular theatre, which working-class audiences saw in their own venues (village halls and so forth).

Other Dreams

Pretty well the only group from the 1960s who are still living the dream of popular theatre created for local communities is Welfare State International. Founded in 1968 by John Fox they create theatre projects 'to order', using carnival, processions, fireworks, dancing and spectacular visual images in their shows.

David EDGAR (b. 1948) wrote plays for the General Will company, targeting the Conservative government. He mainly wrote agit-prop, but moved into socialist realism by the mid 1970s.

The first stage play of *Caryl* CHURCHILL (b. 1938), *Owners* (1972), was, like subsequent plays, motivated by her hatred of social injustice. *Light Shining in Buckinghamshire* (1976) and *Cloud Nine*

1969 BBC television's *Monty Python's Flying Circus* is a series of satirical, anarchic sketches, written and performed by a group of talented young actors.

1972 Charlie Chaplin's *Limelight*, banned in the USA since 1952 because of alleged Communist sympathies, is finally re-released.

1979 Engineer Frank Rudy develops Nike's 'Tailwind', the first air-cushioned trainer.

I wonder how many plays have scenes where men do this? (Churchill's *Cloud Nine*).

PROMPT BOX

A very influential figure of the time, though little remembered now, was Albert Hunt. After working with Peter Brook he went to Bradford College of Arts to teach, where he produced a re-staging of the Russian Revolution with thousands of local residents in the streets (1967), and his own Brechtian play, *John Ford's Cuban Missile Crisis* (1970), with students of the college. They stopped short of executing the faculty, however.

In America, *Ed* BULLINS (b. 1935) was inspired to write by Amiri Baraka's work. He has produced several highly successful plays, like *In the Wine Time* (1968), and *The Fabulous Miss Marie* (1971), which are as much influenced by jazz and blues music as any theatre precedents. *Ntozake* SHANGE (b. 1948) is most famous for *For Colored Girls Who Have Considered Suicide When the Rainbow is Enuf* (1976), an interesting set piece of seven recitations of life experiences.

(1979) explored sexual role-playing, *Serious Money* (1987) savaged the sleazy activities of the City money traders (whether or not the City quaked with fear is a well-kept secret). Unlike so many other 'political' writers, Churchill has avoided pedantry, which gives her work an energy and theatrical variety.

Two coloured girls considering their feet in Ntozake Shange's *For Colored Girls*... .

1963 A hotline is established between Washington and Moscow to try and prevent accidental wars.

1974 Haile Selassie is deposed, ending the Solomonic Dynasty of Ethiopian emperors which proverbially descends from Solomon and the Queen of Sheba.

1976 22 African nations boycott the Montreal Olympics, angered by the presence of New Zealand, which still has ties with South Africa.

1960~1990s

Third World Voices

Apartheid and tyranny

Since the 1970s, economic and social conditions in Third World countries have worsened, creating appalling levels of oppression, poverty and dispossession. Independent of each other, many of the poor of these countries have turned to theatre as a means of political expression. Theatre is accessible to them, allowing perhaps the only voice available (until it gets crushed). The following are merely a tiny example of the vast range of work that has emerged from all over Africa, Asia and the Americas.

Wole Soyinka (1986) after receiving the Nobel Literature Prize.

Probably the most important playwright to come out of Africa has been the Nigerian, *Wole SOYINKA* (b. 1935). His plays – for example, *A Dance of the Forests* (1960), and *A Play of Giants* (1984) – are complex, charting the difficulties faced by Yoruba cultural values in post-colonial Nigeria. In 1977, he produced a Nigerian version of Gay's *Beggar's Opera*, called *Opera Woyonsi*, which attacked Emperor Bokasa.

In South Africa, the white liberal writer *Athol FUGARD* (b. 1932) has claimed his works, from *Boesman and Lena* (1969), through the 'workshop' plays, including *Sizwe Banzi is Dead* (1972), are 'regional' non-political plays about individuals in specific situations.

PROMPT BOX

Augusto Boal wrote a book in 1983 called *The Theatre of the Oppressed* (a subject he is well qualified to discuss). In it he refers to audiences as 'spect-actors', which means they co-create a play by offering different solutions to problems in the text. It's a good idea – we could have Lear tell his daughters to sod off, or Godot finally turn up!

1982 King Sobhuza II of Swaziland dies at the age of 83, the world's longest-reigning monarch.

1990 After 23 years of armed struggle, Namibia wins independence from South Africa and becomes an independent nation.

1995 Nigerian writer and human rights activist Ken Saro-Wiwa, is publicly executed as a political dissident.

Supporting Roles

Throughout South Africa in the 1970s, theatre became the best means for blacks to reassert black nationalism, and their efforts influenced white liberals in existing theatres. Two of the most innovative companies were **The Market Theatre** *in Johannesburg and the* **Space Theatre** *in Cape Town. Both provided venues for Fugard's plays.*

'We three kings.' Athol Fugard and actors from *Sizwe Banzi*.

But they are clearly shaped by events from South Africa's political tensions. He has been attacked for not fully representing the black situation, but what he does very well is to interrogate a broader view of South African society as a whole, which is not only black. The success of *Sizwe Banzi* (based on the problems caused by the apartheid pass laws) and Fugard's 'workshop' methods inspired director Barney Simon and his actors to co-create *Woza Albert (1982)*, which toured the West to great acclaim.

In Brazil during the 1960s particular attention was paid to the success of North American groups like the Living Theatre. American-trained *Augusto* BOAL (b. 1931), began, in 1956, to produce Brecht-inspired political theatre, such as *Revolution in South America* (1961), for the São Paulo Teatro Arena. After 1968, Brazil clamped down on such activities. Boal was tortured and imprisoned. In exile he continued his experiments into 'teatro jornal' (documentary theatre) and 'teatro invisible' (public space theatre) where spectators are unaware a rehearsed performance is happening.

Oppressed Groups

In Jamaica, a group of women have formed the company Sistren to articulate their plight as perhaps the most oppressed class of women in the Third World. They are now known internationally. The theatre project of the Kenyan people of Kamiriithu, led by the playwright Ngugi wa Thiong'o, opposed the Kenyan dictatorship only to have their plays banned, Thiong'o thrown into prison and their theatre bulldozed by the authorities.

1950 The first sex change operation is performed in Denmark. New Yorker George Jorgensen becomes Christine.

1957 Australian novelist, poet and playwright Patrick White's novel, *Voss*, chronicles a Nietzschean German visionary's doomed expedition to cross the continent.

1965 The Merchant-Ivory film *Shakespeare Wallah* follows a troupe of English actors touring India shortly after the end of British colonial rule.

1950~1990s

Awakening Ex-colonies

Australia and Canada

Black Australia has a dance-drama tradition traversing the (estimated) 40,000 years the aborigines have been there. Rituals relating to initiation, magic and tribal ceremonies have been passed down from spiritual ancestors. In white Australia, however, until the 1950s attitudes to the arts were largely divided into either urbanite sycophancy towards all things English, or the anti-art ignorance of the redneck.

Aboriginal dance-dramas tell stories that relate the culture's social life and spiritual beliefs.

The American actor J.C. Williamson dominated Australian theatre management for almost 60 years with imported English or American rubbish. 'Australians don't want Australian' was his justification for not showing the slightest interest in either the country or its people. No one argued because he spiced the general pap he gave theatregoers with just enough 'high culture' to keep the most obsequious (and influential) of them happy. This was why any local talent left just as soon as it could buy a ticket.

The Summer of the Seventeenth Doll (1955) by *Ray Lawler* (b. 1921), is probably still Australia's best known play. It had an immediate and beneficial effect on playwriting, starting a 'school' of three-act Realist plays. In the 1960s a copy of La Mama (see page 127) opened in Melbourne, producing a 'café theatre' company. In 1970 they moved to a local pram factory and changed their name to the Australian Performing Group. Their

1980 In a vote on whether the predominantly French province of Quebec should separate from Canada, 59.9 per cent say no; in 1995 the percentage will be down to 51.

1992 Queen Elizabeth II's 'annus horribilis': two of her sons' marriages end in public scandal and fire breaks out at Windsor Castle. She will be the first British monarch to pay income tax.

1997 Hong Kong becomes a 'special administrative region' of China, in accordance with the terms of the 99-year lease agreed in 1898 between China and Britain.

excellent influence has been crucial in developing a very active and high-quality Australian 'alternative' theatre.

In Canada there exists a clear division between the English-speaking and French-speaking areas (quelle surprise!). As in Australia, early theatre came from colonial masters, though the presence of a competitive French culture and a less isolating geographical position offset the worst effects of this. Companies like Manitoba Theatre Centre (1958) began a regional movement, and Tarragon Theatre (1970s) helped develop an alternative theatre in the English language, but French Canadian culture has produced the most interesting physical, visual and dramatic theatre of the nation. Robert LePage, for example, stunned the world in the 1980s and 1990s with some of the most brilliantly visual theatre ever seen in the West. He is exceptional for his interest in the experience of performance, and works like *The Seven Streams of the River Ola* are performed over several years, changing continually along the way.

Supporting Roles

Patrick White *(1912–90), the Australian novelist, had four plays staged at university theatres in the 1960s. His use of Expressionist styles and almost caricatured characterization opened up new experimental avenues. The French Canadian writer* **Marcel Dubé** *(b. 1930) is the most influential Canadian playwright since 1950, with plays such as* Zone *(1955) and* Private Soldier *(1958).*

'Tit Coq

The modern French Canadian theatre began with the production, in 1948, of *'Tit Coq*, by Gratien Gélinas. Because the play was written in French, and followed the search for identity of its protagonist, it seemed to speak for the whole of post-war French Canada. Its success was phenomenal, with over 500 performances in Québec (only the French could think a title like that was a good idea).

Robert LePage's *Elsinore* (1996), used slide projection and cinematic effects. He played Hamlet (and several other roles) but the star was the gigantic, ever-changing set.

1964 International Tottenham Hotspur soccer-player John White dies after being struck by lightning while sheltering under a tree.

1968 British Conservative MP Enoch Powell attacks the British immigration policy: 'As I look ahead I see the river foaming with much blood.'

1973 American film director, writer and actor Woody Allen directs and stars in his futuristic comedy *Sleeper*.

1964 to the present

Blurring the Boundaries

Post-modernism

'What is this thing called 'post-modernism?', I hear you cry. Well, it's a critic's term, which means real artists and people with blood in their veins ignore it. So should you. The phrase itself can only describe what it isn't, which is modernism, rather than clarify what it is. This vagueness sometimes makes it perfect for describing total rubbish that no one understands, but will pay a lot for because they don't want to appear ignorant. Let's face it, art sometimes brings out the worst in people.

Robert Wilson in Hamlet, 1996. His plays are visually interesting but tedious.

Yawn...
Typical of the Ontological-Hysteric Theatre's productions was *Total Recall* (1970), where emotionless, untrained performers intoned monotonous dialogue, whilst Foreman perched above them, sounding a buzzer every so often. This was done to 'force [audiences] to another level of consciousness'. Richard, dear heart, some of us can barely manage the lowest (like that in which you become aware that you're sitting in a theatre, bored out of your mind).

What's more, all the so-called 'post-modern' elements of pastiche, visible artifice, fiction seen as fiction, crossovers with other popular styles etc. have existed in experimental theatre since at least Alfred Jarry or the Dadaists.

Robert WILSON (b. 1941), American painter and director, constructs a visual theatre. He has worked with brain-damaged children to create dream-like pieces – for example, *A Letter to Queen Victoria* (1974) and *Einstein on the Beach* (1976) – where repetition and slow movement are deliberate. All his opera-like pieces lack conventional plot, character or 'realistic' structures. The sense of time is altered, so crossing the stage can take an hour (watching it can seem like five!).

Behind the Scenes
After the first Robert Wilson production was shown in Europe (*Deafman Glance*, 1970), the Surrealist Louis Aragon wrote enthusiastically to his colleague André Breton, describing it as 'what we from whom Surrealism was born dreamt would arise after us, beyond us...'. So the tradition continues. But perhaps the letter was a Surrealist irony....

1979 There are 21,456 murders reported in the States, more than half of which involved handguns.

1986 Corazon Aquino is elected President of the Philippines, ousting Ferdinand Marcos; he and his shoe-buying wife Imelda have bled the country of an estimated 45 billion over 20 years.

1997 Mother Teresa, the Albanian-born nun who dedicated her life to caring for the poor of Calcutta, dies in the same week as Princess Diana.

Willem Dafoe was a regular in Wooster Group productions.

Richard FOREMAN (b. 1937) started his Ontological-Hysteric Theatre in 1968. His intention, it seems, was to explore ontology (metaphysical science concerned with the state of 'being'). The 'hysteric' bit refers not to the name of the theatre company, but to 'classic middle-class, boulevard theatre... hysteric in its psychological topology' (oh well, that's all right, then).

Arianne MNOUCHKINE (b. 1934) creates collaborative pieces with her company, Théâtre du Soleil. Based on a mixture of Artaud and Brecht (now, that's living dangerously!), where both social problems and private angst could be examined, her creations include *The Clowns* (1969) and *Mephisto* (1979).

Arianne Mnouchkine's shows were invariably controversial.

Out of the Performance Group (see page 126) came the Wooster Group, under *Elizabeth* LECOMPTE (b. 1944). Works like *Rumstick Road* (1977), or *L.S.D.* (1984), were based either on the autobiographical splurges of company member Spalding Gray, or the writings of Timothy Leary with a bit of Miller's *The Crucible* thrown in (which Miller hated).

Théâtre du Soleil's Martine Frank: is she perhaps allergic to her make-up?

1962 Rachel Carson publishes *The Silent Spring*, warning of the dangers of pesticide use for wildlife.

1972 Deranged Australian Laszlo Tuth attacks and damages Michelangelo's Pietà in Rome.

1988 *Daedalus 88*, a man-powered aircraft, flies 74 miles over the Aegean.

1961 to the present

Full Circle at Fin de Siècle?

Theatre returns to ritual and dance

As with all art after Modernism, what happens next? Sometimes it seems as if we've seen it, been there, done it, watched the video and bought the T-shirt – or scrounged it at the press showing. But in a sense it's always been like that. Each new development has necessitated further new development. As the realities of life grow more complex, so does our need for, and methods of, expressing them.

The actor as mannequin.

Theatre in the West may well be dying in terms of 'plays': the average age of audiences on Broadway is 45 and only about seven per cent of the population of Britain regularly see theatre at all, whilst films and television thrive and interactive entertainments grow fast. Even in the East, traditional theatres like nō are losing audiences to film. But in the Third World theatre is still seen as a way of voicing political

Mime

Mime, which meant a form of comic folk play to the Ancient Greeks and was then used to describe the performer, became a silent art in France during the eighteenth century, when dramatic monopoly stopped fairground 'actors' from speaking. It has since developed through Jean-Louis Barrault, Marcel Marceau and, in the US, Bread and Puppet Theatre. 1960's intellectuals from Greenwich Village prized Marcel Marceau soundtrack albums as vital lifestyle props.

Jerome Savary's grand *Magic Circus* (1975), using traditional 'types' from European theatre.

1996 Earvin 'Magic' Johnson, having retired from basketball because he was HIV positive, makes a sensational comeback with the Los Angeles Lakers.

1997 Scientists at the Roslin Institute in Edinburgh announce the first cloned sheep, Dolly, created from the tissue of an adult ewe.

1998 A tape of American President Bill Clinton's testimony to the Grand Jury on his sexual relationship with White House intern Monica Lewinsky is shown on television around the world.

concerns in ways the West has given up. Also, perhaps Western 'live performance' can only travel in a non-realistic direction now, as exemplified by Eugenio Barba, Jerome Savary, Peter Brook, Wilson, Foreman and others of the avant-garde.

Eugenio BARBA (b. 1936) worked with Jerzy Grotowsky before founding the Odin Teatret, based in Holstebrö in Denmark. Odin is a centre for theatre research as well as a performing company, and a focus for the International School of Theatre Anthropology. Barba has published his ideas in *The Floating Islands* (1984) and *Beyond The Floating Islands* (1986). In France, *Jerome* SAVARY (b. 1942), co-founded the Grand Théâtre Panique in the 1960s, which became the Grand Magic Circus after 1968. They produce highly successful, subversive part cabaret, part social satires usually in non-theatre spaces.

Peter BROOK (b. 1925) began at Birmingham Rep in the 1940s, moving on to the Royal Shakespeare Company 20 years later. Never content with traditional practices, he has moved ever onwards and upwards. Of course, as he became more imaginative and challenging, he had to leave Britain, so he moved to Paris, opening an International Centre for Theatre Research. His international company have performed productions including *The Conference of the Birds* (1976), and a nine-hour epic retelling of the entire Indian *Mahabharata* (1985) – and worth every one of the 32,400 seconds.

Supporting Roles

Tadeutz Kantor *(b. 1915) the Polish director and painter, formed a group of artists called Cricot II, in 1956. He has since produced happenings and theatre pieces using actors as props and mannequins (and props and mannequins as actors?). He later developed the Theatre of Death with performances like seances.* **Pina Bausch** *explored sexual roles through mime and dance with her Wuppertal Tanztheater.*

Glossary

Get the vocab right! You don't wear an apron, live in a flat or tidy your lawn with a rake.

ALIENATION EFFECT
Any device used to help the audience perceive the stage 'world' objectively as storytelling, thus stopping them from emotionally identifying with a character (e.g. visible stagehands or actors announcing who they are going to play).

AMPHITHEATRE
An outdoor theatre, like a half bowl with semi-circular seating sloping down to the stage area. They have excellent acoustics.

ANGELS
Financial backers of a production.

APRON
Part of a stage which projects out towards the audience.

ARENA THEATRE
Originally the oval Roman amphitheatres where audience surrounded the stage area.

BEGINNERS
1) Those actors who appear first on stage.
2) A call given by stage managers to get them there (five minutes before curtain).

BOX SET
A set of three sides – mainly used to imitate a room (the audience looks through an imaginary 'fourth wall').

BUSINESS
Activities invented by 'realist' actors to reinforce character (e.g. nervously fiddling with things), or to make them look as if they know why they're there.

CORPSE
Uncontrollable giggling by actors on stage (used as a verb – to corpse): caused by a) drunkenness, b) nervousness, c) forgetfulness, d) the sudden realization that the play is dreadful.

CUE-TO-CUE
Technical rehearsal to allow the crew to work through all the cues (lighting, scene changes etc.)

CYCLORAMA
A plain screen extending around the performing space for image projection or simply to give a feeling of infinite space.

DARK
A term used to describe a theatre closed to the public, even temporarily.

DEUS EX MACHINA
An event or person who 'appears' in the nick of time to save a situation (originally Greek – 'The god in the machine', where gods were suspended above the stage ready to descend).

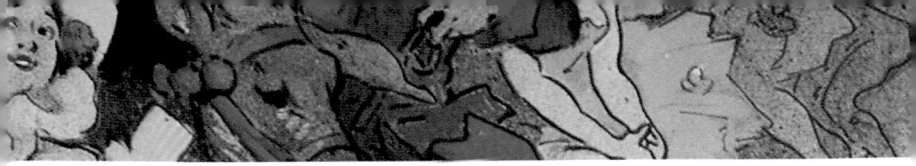

DIORAMA
A three-dimensional illusion created by painted cloth and cleverly focused lights.

DOWNSTAGE
Part of stage closest to the audience.

DRESS REHEARSAL
The final rehearsal before opening, originally intended to ensure all costumes were finished. It is also, as Alfred Jarry noted: '…a free show for a select group of artists and friends of the author, and where for one unique evening the audience is almost expurgated of idiots'.

FLAT
An element of scenery made of a wooden frame covered in painted canvas or plywood.

FOOTLIGHTS
A batten of lights on the edge of the stage. First used around 1670, but no longer necessary.

FOURTH WALL
An imaginary wall between audience and players.

GREEN ROOM
A room near the stage for actors to rest and exchange gossip.

PRINCIPALS
The lead actors in a play.

PROSCENIUM ARCH
An archway, or division, between auditorium and stage.

RAKE
An area of stage sloping down to the audience to improve sightlines.

ROSTRUM
A piece of portable staging. Usually a box-like platform which might link to other rostra to raise parts of the action.

RUN-THROUGH
A rehearsal where all the bits of a production are put in the right order. Better known as a 'stagger through'.

STAGE LEFT
Left-hand side from the cast's view. Stage Right is the opposite.

SUBTEXT
A set of meanings lurking beneath the 'surface' meaning of a play that are usually and mysteriously only known to the director.

THEATRE IN THE ROUND
Any auditorium where the audience sits around a central stage.

THRUST STAGE
Staging that projects into the audience so they sit on either side.

UPSTAGE
The part of the stage furthest from the audience, or – as a verb – the time-honoured practice of scene-stealing.

WINGS
Areas at the side of the stage hidden from the audience's view.

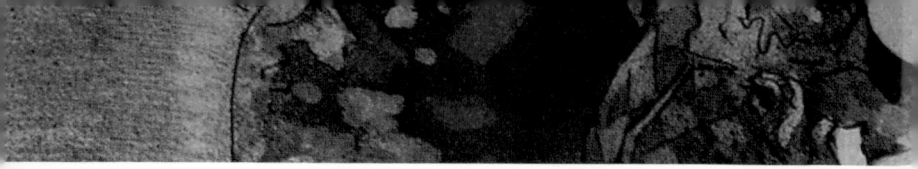

Old Thespian Sayings and Superstitions

Actors are under a lot of pressure, darling, with all those beastly lines to learn, costumes that aren't always as flattering as they should be and directors that make Hitler seem like Mother Teresa. They have their own little ways of coping.

BREAK A LEG
Traditionally a good-luck greeting between thespians.

FALL DOWN BACKWARD
Another thespian good-luck greeting.

FIRE
Unlucky word in theatre generally. This is from the time when candles and gas were used and often sent the building up in flames. Hence 'fireproofing' is the First Commandment for technicians.

FRIBBLE
A word used to describe the ad libbing actors did when they forgot lines in the seventeenth century. These days it's simply called 'drivel'.

MACBETH
Unlucky to speak this name or quote from the play in a theatre. The play has been dogged by bad luck since the boy actor playing Lady Macbeth died as it opened in 1606. It is always referred to as 'The Scottish Play' instead.

ONION AT THE END
A music hall term meaning any action/lines at the end of a play designed to get the audience crying.

SKIN OFF YOUR NOSE
19th-century thespian good-luck greeting. Coarse make-up would literally peel skin from an actor's face after a performance; so 'Skin off your nose' meant 'Hope you stay in work'!

SPIT AND DRIBBLE
The cheapest seats in the house, usually on the highest balcony from where wags would spit and dribble on wealthier theatregoers below.

THE OLD COMPLAINT
A thespian euphemism for drunkenness.

WHISTLING
Bad luck to whistle whilst in the Green Room. If you do, you must turn around three times, leave the room for one minute, knock three times and re-enter! Not a good idea if you're suffering from 'the old complaint'.

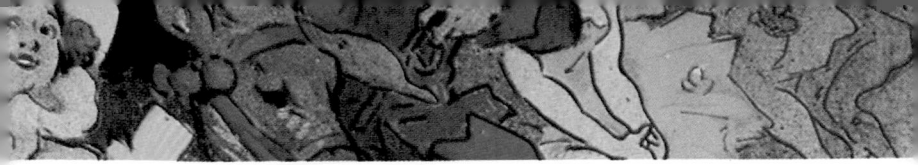

Notable Performances

Some shows quietly close after a few weeks or transfer swiftly to the sticks. A few go down in the annals (yes, I said ann-a-l-s) of time and create theatre history – although not always for the right reasons.

BREAKING NEW GROUND

Don't you wish you'd seen Stanislavsky's first collaboration with Chekhov – *The Seagull* at the Moscow Art Theatre, 1896? Or the première of Beckett's *Waiting for Godot* in Paris in 1953? Or the day snoozing British theatre woke up to John Osborne's *Look Back in Anger* in 1956?

GENDER ISSUES

When Margaret Hughes played Desdemona in 1660, she was the first professional actress in British theatre.

'I DIED OUT THERE, DARLING!'

In *Le Mystère du Nouveau Testament* at Valenciennes, 1547, the actor playing the Devil was gutted and hanged by mistake.

The author and lead actor, Molière, died on stage during a production of *The Imaginary Invalid*, Comédie Française, Paris, 1673.

On 14 April 1865, President Lincoln was shot by an actor, John Wilkes Booth, while watching *Our American Cousin* at Ford's Theatre in Washington.

TECHNICAL HITCHES

The first-ever production of *Henry VIII*, 29 June, 1613, resulted in the Globe Theatre burning to the ground (see page 35).

The 1912 *Hamlet* at the Moscow Arts Theatre was memorable because Craig's gigantic set collapsed.

Hair, London 1966, marked the first time a penis had been seen on the British stage.

WHAT A RIOT!

Plays that have inspired the audience to riot include Jarry's *Ubu Roi*, Paris, 1896, and Synge's *Playboy of the Western World*, New York, 1911.

WHEN'S THE INTERVAL?

Peter Brook's *Mahabarata*, Avignon, 1985, lasted for nine hours.

Ken Cambell directed *The Warp*, Edinburgh, 1979 lasting 24 hours.

John Arden's *The Non-Stop Connolly Show* (1975) took 26½ hours to perform in the Irish Republic's capital, Dublin.

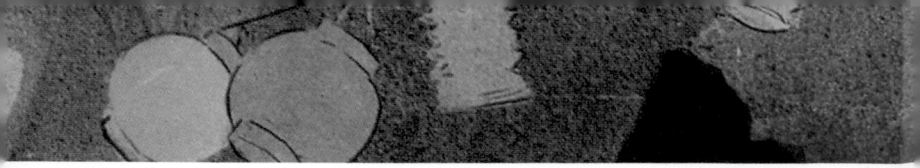

Index

Aeschyllus 16–17
Africa 130–1
agit-prop 128–9
Alfieri, Vittorio 63
America 68–71, 86–7, 96–7, 124–5
Andreini, Giovan Battista 51
Antoine, André 79
Appia, Adolphe 104
Aretino, Pietro 25
Aristotle 12, 16
Artaud, Antonin 110–11
Asia, South-east 54–5
Australia 132–3
Ayckbourn, Alan 121

Ball, Hugo 106
Bancroft, Squire 75
Baraka, Amiri 123
Barba, Eugenio 137
Barrie, J.M. 101
Beaumarchais, Pierre-Augustin Caron 60
Beaumont, Francis 37
Beckett, Samuel 112–13
Bel Geddes, Norman 97
Belasco, David 97
Bergerac, Cyrano de 40–1, 90–1
Bernhardt, Sarah 78–9
Bird, Robert Montgomery 71
Blok, Alexandr 91
Boal, Augusta 130–1
Booth, Edwin 71
Boucicault, Dion 75, 86
Brecht, Bertholt 109
Brenton, Howard 128
Brook, Peter 137
Browne, Robert 48
Büchner, Georg 76
Bullins, Ed 129
Burbage, James 32, 35

Calderón de la Barca, Pedro 29
Camus, Albert 112–13
Canada 133
Cervantes, Miguel 29
Chekhov, Anton 85
China 56–7
Churchill, Caryl 128–9
Cibber, Colley 66
Colum, Padraic 103
commedia dell'arte 26–7
Cooper, Thomas Abthorpe 69
Corneille, Pierre 40–1
Coward, Noel 116
Craig, (Edward) Gordon 104

Dada 106
D'Annunzio, Gabriele 80–1
D'Avenant, William 44
Devine, George 120
Diderot, Denis 60
Drew, Mrs 71
Duse, Eleonora 81

Edgar, David 128
Egyptians 14–15
Euripides 16–17
Evreinov, Nikolai 91
existentialism 112–13
expressionism 98–9

Fastnachtsspiel 46–7
Felix, Elisa (Rachel) 78
Fennell, James 69
Fletcher, John 37
Fo, Dario 123
Foreman, Richard 134–5
Forrest, Edwin 70
France 40–3, 60–1, 78–9, 90–1
Fugard, Athol 130–1
futurism 92–3

Galsworthy, John 101
Garrick, David 66–7
Germany 46–7, 64–5, 76–7
Gielgud, John 118
Goethe, Johann Wolfgang von 64–5
Gogol, Nikolai 84
Goldoni, Carlo 62–3
Gorky, Maksim 95
Gozzi, Carlo 63
Granville-Baker, Harley 100
Greeks 16–17
Greene, Robert 33, 35
Gregory, Augusta 102
Griboyedov, Alexander 84
Grotowsky, Jerzy 111
Gwyn, Nell 44–5

Hardy, Alexandre 40
Hare, David 128
Hauptmann, Gerhart 94
Henslowe, Philip 34
Horniman, Annie 102
Hughes, Langston 124
Hugo, Victor 78

Ibsen, Henrik 82–3
India 52–3
Ionescu, Eugène 113
Ireland 102–3
Irving, Henry 74–5
Italy 24–7, 50–1, 62–3, 80–1

Japan 58–9
Jarry, Alfred 106–7
Jones, Inigo 38–9
Jonson, Ben 33, 38–9

Kaiser, Georg 99
Kazan, Elia 114–15
Kean, Edmund 72
Kemble, Charles 72
Kemble, Fanny 72
Kemble, John Philip 67
Kempe, Will 48
Killigrew, Thomas 44
Kiyotsugu, Kwanami 59
Klinger, Friedrich Maximillian von 64–5
Kokoschka, Oscar 99

Lawler, Ray 132
LeCompte, Elizabeth 135
Lorca, Federico García 107
Lugné-Poe, Aurelian 90

McGrath, John 128
Machiavelli, Niccolò 25
Macready, William 74
Maeterlinck, Maurice 90
Mamet, David 125
Manzoni, Alessandro 81
Marinetti, Filippo T. 92–3
Marlowe, Christopher 32–3
Marston, John 37
masques 38–9
Mayakovsky, Vladimir 93
Method acting 114–15
Meyerhold, Vsevolod 108
Middleton, Thomas 37
Miller, Arthur 124–5
mime 136
Mnouchkine, Arianne 135
Molière, Jean-Baptiste Poquelin 42–3
Moralities 21
Motokiyu, Seami 59
Musset, Alfred de 78
Mystery Cycles 21–3

nationalism 80–1
Naturalism 74–7, 94–5
Nemirovich-Danchenko, Vladimir 89
Norton, Thomas 31

O'Casey, Sean 103
Odets, Clifford 97
Olivier, Laurence 119
O'Neill, Eugene 95, 99
Orton, Joe 123
Osborne, John 120

passion plays 14–15
Payne, John 70
Performance Group 126
Phelps, Samuel 74
Pinter, Harold 123
Pirandello, Luigi 107
Piscator, Erwin 108–9
Plautus 19
post-modernism 134–5
puppet plays 54–5
Pushkin, Alexandr 84

Rachel *see* Felix, Elise
Racine, Jean 41
Rattigan, Terence 116–17
Realism 74–5, 80, 96–7
Richardson, Ralph 118–19
Ristori, Adelaide 81
ritual 12–13
Robertson, Tom 75
Robson, Flora 119
Romans 18–19
Romanticism 78–9
Rostand, Edmond 79, 90–1
Rowley, Thomas 37
Russia 84–5, 91

Sachs, Hans 47
Sackville, Thomas 31
Salvini, Tommaso 81
Sardou, Victorien 75
Sartre, Jean-Paul 112
Savary, Jerome 137
Saxe-Meinengen, George, Duke of 76
Scandinavia 82–3
Schiller, Friedrich 65
Schlemmer, Oscar 107
Scribe, Eugène 75
Seneca 19
shadow plays 54–5
Shakespeare, William 34–5
Shange, Ntozake 129
Shaw, George Bernard 100–1
Shepard, Sam 125
Sheridan, Richard Brinsley 67
Sherriff, R. C. 117
Siddons, Sarah 67
Sophocles 16–17
Soyinka, Wole 130
Spain 28–9
Stanislavsky, Konstantin 88–9
Strasberg, Lee 114–15
Strindberg, August 82–3
symbolism 90–1
Synge, J. M. 102–3

Tagore, Rabindranath 53
Terence 19
Terry, Ellen 74–5
Thespis 17
Toller, Ernst 99
Tolstoy, Leo Nikolayevitch 84–5
Tourneur, Cyril 37
Travers, Ben 117
Tzara, Tristan 106

Udall, Nicholas 31

Vega, Lope 29
Vestris, Lucia 72
Voltaire, François-Marie Arouet 60–1

Wagner, Richard 77
Webster, John 36–7
Wedekind, Frank 98–9
Wesker, Arnold 120–1
Wilde, Oscar 101
Williams, Tennessee 124
Wilson, Robert 134

Yeats, W.B. 102–3

Zola, Emile 79, 96

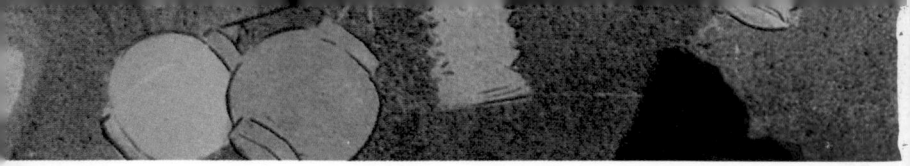

PHOTOGRAPHIC CREDITS

Archiv für Kunst und Geschicte, London: 18, 19, 22, 23 (Staatliche Kunstsammlugen Kassel), 25 (Pallazo Vecchio, Florence), 29 (SMPK Nationalgalerie, Berlin), 30 (Sherborne Castle, Dorset), 39 (Schloss Augustusburg Bruhl), 64 (Goethe Gallerie), 65 (Gemaldie von Anton Graff), 76, 78, 94, 95B, 96, 102 (Hugh Lane Municipal Gallery), 107 (Buhnen Archiv Oskar Schlemmer), 124T, 134.

AKG, London/Herbert Kraft: 12/13B.

AKG, London/Eric Lessing: 13, 26, 27, (Louvre, Paris), 60 (Chateau Ferney-Voltaire).

AKG, London/Jean Louis-Nou: 53 (Asiatic Society of Bombay).

The Bridgeman Art Library: 24 (Villa Farnesina, Rome), 28 (Phillips Fine Art), 32 (Corpus Christi College, Cambridge), 43 (Victoria and Albert Museum), 48 (Phillips Fine Art), 55 (British Museum), 56 (Stapleton College), 62 (Casa Goldoni, Venice), 63T (Galleria degli Uffizi), 70 (Museum of the City of New York), 83 (Nasjonal Galleriet, Oslo), 106 (Phillips Fine Art).

BAL/Roger Viollet: 40 (Musée du Breuil de St. Germain, Langres).

Corbis, London: 98 (Robbie Jack), 89 (Austrian Archive).

Corbis-Bettman: 80, 99, 115T, 129 (UPI).

e. t. archive, London: 17, 35, 44, 46, 50, 66, 68, 72, 73.

Hulton Getty, London: 92, 93, 110T (H. Guttman), 110B, 118, 119, 120 (Polkington), 122, 131, 136 (Fred Mott).

Magnum/Martine Franck: 135B, 135R.

Performing Arts Library, London: 33, 61, 76T.

PAL/Clive Barda: 63B.

PAL/Henrietta Butler: 103.

PAL/Ben Christopher: 109, 111, 128.

PAL/Fritz Curzon: 117.

PAL/Ivan Kinci: 43R.

PAL/Michael Ward: 97.

PAL/John Wender: 54.

Rex Features: 114, 119, 123T, 123B, 124B, 130, 132, 135T.

The Stock Market, London: 57, 58, 85.

Emmanuel Valette/courtesy of Cultural Industries: 133.

Reg Wilson, London: Title page, 11, 36, 37, 41, 49, 59, 82, 85, 90, 95T, 112, 121, 125, 126, 127.

COPYRIGHT

p. 106 Jean Miro: Poster for *Ubu Roi* – play by Alfred Jarry. **© DACS 1999**

p.107 Oskar Schlemmer: Design for costumes for Triadic Ballet. **© C. Raman Schlemmer**